FOREVER PURRFECT

A true account of an extraordinary cat
and the lessons he taught me.

Benito Cossari

First published in Australia by Aurora House

This edition published in Australia by Aurora House 2023
www.aurorahouse.com.au
Copyright © Benito Cossari 2023

Typesetting and e-book design: Cognition Technology |
www.cognition-technology.in
Cover Designer: Donika Mishineva | www.artofdonika.com

ISBN number: 978-1-922913-29-6 (paperback)

A catalogue record for this
book is available from the
NATIONAL LIBRARY OF AUSTRALIA   National Library of Australia

Distributed by: *Ingram Content*: www.ingramcontent.com
Australia: *Phone*: +613 9765 4800 |
Email: lsiaustralia@ingramcontent.com
Milton Keynes UK: *Phone*: +44 (0)845 121 4567 |
Email: enquiries@ingramcontent.com
La Vergne, TN USA: *Phone*: +1 800 509 4156 |
Email: inquiry@lightningsource.com

Dedication

Sylvester's story is dedicated to every animal that has blessed the homes of humans around the world with their unconditional love and companionship and the lasting legacy they leave behind.

Acknowledgement

A special thank you to Megan Crocombe.
Your high standards with editing and your precision with
the English language is greatly appreciated.

Donika Mishineva, thank you for designing a great cover.
You've captured Sylvester perfectly.

Georgina Holmes, thank you for your assistance in the
production of Forever Purrfect.

Justine Joffe, thank you for your proofreading and
feedback.

Contents

Foreword

As a Veterinarian, I have treated many pets and their owners over the years.

For some owners, their pet is an integral part of their life, a pal for their children and a surrogate child for themselves. Rarely have I seen the commitment between an owner and their pet like the one Ben and Sylvester shared.

Without Ben and his family's devotion, Sylvester would have passed away in the first instance with his severe blood loss.

For a while, things improved, and then new threats and illnesses presented themselves.

Ben never lost hope, and Sylvester did everything he could to stay as long as possible in this life.

This was truly a special bond between a man and his cat.

I was privileged to be a small part of their extraordinary journey.

Dr. Alison Brown, BVSc Hons.

Introduction

"Until one has loved an animal, a part of one's soul remains unawakened."
Anatole France (1844-1924).

Does this resonate with you? For me, its meaning captures the essence of this story and it's why it's the opening line of this book. If you've been touched by the love of an animal, then it ought to have meaning for you too.

If I could speak with Anatole France today, I'd say to him, "Perfectly written." My soul has awakened because of the love of an animal. A black and white cat named Sylvester.

Even though this quote was penned a few centuries ago, its suggestion is timeless; the unadulterated spirit of an animal and the love they give is precious. If you've been touched by an animal's grace, then Sylvester's story is for you. I know the tales of a human and an animal inescapably lead to the same emotional outcome. Yours may differ with circumstances, place and time, but I'm sure the gift of unconditional love will remain the same.

Unmistakably, animals have an uncanny way of reaching into our hearts, pulling on our heart strings and then surreptitiously holding on for eternity. As blessings in disguise, pets come into our lives at just the right time; some stay for a little while, others stay for a length of time.

In every calling, our animal friends show us the exemplary way to cope with the volatile, sometimes heartless and cruel world. Their loyalty is indisputable and their companionship is sacred. The expression that typifies a human and a dog's relationship, 'Man's best friend', is also appropriate for Sylvester and me. I imagine it is for you and your beloved pet as well.

I experienced a myriad of emotions and lessons throughout Sylvester's life. By reading our story, you'll go on an emotional journey through the highs and lows, and end with the knowledge and wisdom that animals are indeed teachers as much as they are a cat, dog, bird or mouse. I anticipate you'll be enlightened by Sylvester and fall in love with his personality, as I did for all those years.

I'm hopeful this book provides a deeper understanding and awareness of your pet's extraordinary personality and the life lessons they offer you.

I've written our story from two viewpoints; my experience and perspective of our journey and Sylvester's, fictionally conveyed through my interpretation. I couldn't think of a better way to take you on this journey. My story, his story—our story—hopefully provides you with the belief that all will be okay somehow and in some way.

May you and your pet have the most blessed life together as I have had with Sylvester.

"All creatures great and small, God made them all."
Traditional Saying

1

Shop Front Window

Upon reflection, it seems such a long time ago. My memory has become vague, but my emotions remain unwavering. It was a defining day that triggered the awakening of my soul and the prelude to a journey that would be filled with immense joy. A diminutive black and white kitten came into my world. A kitten I'd name Sylvester.

It was a warm, humid Friday afternoon in late spring when, unbeknownst to me at the time, serendipity would play a role in the direction of my life. The events that unfolded inevitably altered the course of my life, albeit for the better.

I'd decided to go shopping at a local shopping centre. It was your typical shopping mall with retail shops galore and many food outlets. It had a pet shop situated on the ground level just near the food court. Casually browsing, with no intention to purchase anything, I walked towards the pet shop. I stopped momentarily and gazed through the shop front window. I saw a litter of kittens. There were four kittens in all; a tabby kitten sleeping in its makeshift bed and three boisterous kittens that played fervently with a miniature red rubber ball, each kitten defiant with the other two to attain command of the ball. One of the three frolicking kittens instantly caught my attention. It was playful and small compared to the other three kittens.

It had the most adorable face. It was black with a splash of white from cheek to cheek and a bit more white splashed in between its beautiful big green eyes and above its bright pink nose. Its coat was black with white front paws and white hind legs, and its tail was black from end to end. I wasn't sure if it was male or female, but nonetheless it was the kitten I instantly felt a connection with, so I went inside the store to find out more.

The female assistant, who was stacking shelves with cans of dog food adjacent to the litter of kittens, said to me, "That litter arrived yesterday. Many people have already shown interest in adopting the kittens".

I contemplated momentarily whether to adopt the kitten on the spot. But I'd not come out today to randomly adopt a kitten, so I decided to think about the idea over the weekend, and if by Monday morning the kitten was still available, I'd adopt it.

Throughout the weekend, I couldn't stop thinking about the little black and white kitten. I hoped the kitten was still at the pet store and that no one had come along after I had left and adopted it.

The weekend dragged. I wished it would go quickly; but time seemed to stand still. To distract myself from staring at the clock, I endeavoured to occupy my mind with various tasks; cleaning up my room, reading motivational books, working out at the local gym and watching some movies on TV.

I was twenty something and living with my parents and my younger brother, in a two-story brick veneer house in a beautiful leafy suburb east of the city centre. My mum, kind and caring, would always maintain an impeccably clean house. She loved to look after her family always cooking the tastiest home-style Italian food—the best kind that's only matched by my nonna's cooking, passed down from our ancestors in a village in Southern Italy. My dad treasured all things Italian: politics, history, culture, food. Anything with the Italian flag colours of green, white and red in its D.N.A. he was all for it. My brother, a few years younger than me, always an avid fan of sports; in particular Australian Rules football. I think he'd like a kitten in the house too, but I hadn't said anything to him or my parents about my chance encounter.

Whatever daily task I put my focus on, I'd inevitably return to the uncomfortable thought that the diminutive kitten might have been adopted by somebody else.

Monday morning finally arrived; I awoke at the crack of dawn. I gathered my thoughts and readied myself to travel to the pet shop. It was a short drive from home. My heart beat faster than usual as I started the car engine. The thought that I was too late to adopt the kitten crossed my mind as the engine cranked over. I was overly anxious; negotiating my way through traffic seemed to take forever.

I parked as close as possible to the pet shop and walked towards the entrance of the shopping centre. My heart was beating faster than before. I fretted that I'd squandered a once in a lifetime opportunity and anticipated the disappointment I'd feel in a few moments time when I arrived at the pet store to discover the kitten was no longer there.

I'd worked myself up into a state of extreme apprehension; my head was feeling light and my mouth was dry. My steps morphed into a slight trot as I turned the corner and headed towards the front window display of the pet store. I could see the kittens frolicking in their playpen. My eyes scanned the litter searching for the kitten. As with any life changing events, the seconds seemed like minutes, and the minutes seemed like days. Then, my eyes fixed on the black and white kitten...

It was still there! I sighed with relief as I took a deep breath. Feeling jubilant, I walked into the pet store and spoke with the assistant who was standing near the playpen. A thought flashed through my mind: what if the kitten was already reserved for adoption? I had a sinking feeling in my stomach. Overwhelmed and shaking, I uttered, "Good morning," to the lady standing behind the counter. I asked her if I could hold the black and white kitten. It was sitting in the corner of the playpen gazing at me.

She picked up the kitten and brought it over to me. I asked the question. She immediately responded, "Definitely, the kitten is available to adopt".

I was relieved to hear her response; there was no stopping me now. "Is it male or female?"

"It's a male; he's been here for a couple of days. We call him Socks," she said, as the kitten attempted to jump out of her clasp.

"I'd like to adopt him please." I was euphoric. The build-up of negative emotions throughout the weekend had vanished in an instant.

Moments later, I was holding him. He wriggled, trying to break free. He was probably wondering what all the fuss was about. His eyes inquisitively scanned the room. Before we said our goodbyes, I made sure he had the necessary essentials to feel comfortable in his new home.

I chose a snug bed made out of straw; it reminded me of a woven basket that you'd place bread or fruit into. I also bought food and water bowls and, most importantly, nutritious food; I bought plenty of that for him. The shop assistant placed him gently into a cat carrier so I could carry him safely back home.

Arriving home, I was nervous. What would Mum and Dad think? I know my brother would be happy to have a kitten. My parents on the other hand, not so much. Recently, I'd hinted that I'd love a kitten. Their response was lukewarm at best. But today I was wagering they'd come round when they saw the kitten and would welcome him into our family.

My mum was in the kitchen. Walking towards her, I held the kitten close to my chest then carefully placed him onto the kitchen floor. Mum had her back turned, facing the kitchen sink. Hearing my footsteps, she turned around and looked directly at the kitten walking across the floor. She said with a controlled, but somewhat irritated voice, "I hope you're ready for the responsibility." My dad said little as he walked in from the patio.

On the other hand, my brother, overhearing my discussion with Mum, dashed from his bedroom to the kitchen. He looked at me with a big smirk on his face, saying not a word. He didn't need to. I read his mind: he was elated. He then proceeded to play with the kitten. I told them it was a boy. A few weeks ago, I'd had a daydream that I adopted a black and white kitten. It was a male with a pink nose. I'd prayed with a deep sense of knowing that it would come my way someday. In the following weeks, my inner voice kept whispering to me that I'd indeed have the kitten I prayed for, but I hadn't expected it to happen so soon. I certainly had never thought, the day I went to the shops, that I'd cross paths with this imagined kitten. But I did. I was overjoyed and excited, but most of all thankful.

I prepared the kitten's food. I opened the cat food tin, the first of many that would follow in the years ahead. I poured the chicken and gravy pieces into his new bowl whilst watching him investigate his new surroundings. He sniffed the floor and vetted curiously each of his new family members. They passed his inspection and had his seal of approval. His focus turned to the food sitting in his bowl and thereafter the maze of corridors that lay before him.

The next day I decided on a name for him. Many names came to mind including Socks (the name the pet shop had given him), Magpie (after my favourite football club. Their team colours are black and white, like him) and Righty (paying homage to a cat we once loved called Lefty), but the one that stuck was Sylvester. It was a perfect fit. He resembled a cat I'd known with the same name. The question remained, was he to be as mischievous? Only time would tell. My kitten had a new home, and I had a new friend.

2

Machines That Bite

I like my new home. I have a comfortable bed, plenty of delicious food, fresh water and a loving family.

My human friend is very caring. His name is Ben. He checks on me regularly to see if I need food to eat and water to drink. He calls me Sylvester. I like that name.

I hide from him in places he can't reach. He throws a blue rubber ball to coax me out from under the bed. I can never resist the temptation, so I hurry out from my hiding place and whack the ball back and forth between my paws as I run up and down the hallway.

I find joy running up and down the stairs and through to the lounge room; darting in and out and in between the adjoining sofas. I'm always surprising my human family with bursts of energy when they least expect it. I prepare my attacks on them, ready to pounce, as they relax in the lounge room. I'm faster than any of them; I strike their hands with my paw as they attempt to grab me. I hide in between the connecting sofas for safe measure. Each time I take a jab with my paw, my razor-sharp claws scratch their hands. When an opportunity comes to escape, I run and find a new place to hide, ready for my next chance to pounce on them. My instincts are ever-present. I remember when my brother and I used to play together. We'd fight and scratch, bite and tumble over in the play pen. I miss him. I hope he's found a loving home.

But my favourite activity of the day is sleeping. Actually, come to think of it, it's eating; hmmm... maybe it's playing... I guess I like to do all of these things. But mostly I like spending time with my new family. They're kind and caring towards me. Especially Ben's mum. She's my human mum. Her name is Rose.

As I've settled into my new life, I've become acquainted with my new surroundings. I'm content and comfortable in my new home. I discover new adventures within each room of the house, encountering plenty of bits and pieces to play with. In the lounge room, there are curtains draped to the floor and within my reach to pull down from the curtain rails. Not all the adventures are happy ones though. I've learned to keep away from the monster that crawls along the carpet making an endless wail. It will never be my friend.

Sometimes when this wicked monster crawls across the carpet, its presence frightens me. As soon as I hear it come out of its hiding place, I dash for cover in a safe place. When it commences its hunt, it makes a loud whining noise and, with its long neck and open mouth, it consumes anything in its path. I can hear it growling as it makes its way through the lounge room, then across the bedroom floors. I'm worried it wants to eat me.

Until I know it's disappeared back into its fortress, I wait patiently, hoping its hunt is quick and it goes away. When it becomes silent, I come out of hiding and survey my environment. When the coast is clear, I muster up the courage to head back out on my adventures across the domains of each room throughout the house. The monster is the scariest object in my house. I don't like it.

I see a fly dancing above the surface of the kitchen floor. It looks like it's skating on ice as it glides gracefully, twirling and spinning over the smooth ceramic floor tiles. I'm tempted to swipe it with my claws, but I'm feeling merciful and refrain from killing and eating the unassuming buzzing insect. I let it fly away. I'm excited and curious with each passing day; it's a smorgasbord of fun and frivolity.

I have a bed with a warm, comfy blanket in a room just for me. This is where I fall asleep at night. I have an endless supply of food; my food bowl is always full to the brim. In the corner of my room, I have a kitty litter tray.

I love to explore my new home and its contents, at the same time I'd like to get to know my new family a whole lot better. But right now, it's time to rest for the night; I will cuddle up in my bed and doze right off to sleep. Tomorrow is another day of adventures for me.

3
The Golden Rule

There's a limited window of opportunity to revel in the enjoyment of having a kitten enrich your home. The time goes quickly and too soon the kitten matures into an adult.

In a matter of months, Sylvester grew in size and in self-confidence. He was mischievous and at times disobedient. If we didn't establish rules, we were sure he'd run amok. Mum, in particular, taught him to obey these rules. She didn't want to adopt another cat. She'd become emotionally attached to our previous cats and if another untimely passing were to happen it would be too much for her to bear. To add, she was fastidious about cleanliness and keeping things in order. Having Sylvester to care for and clean up after now meant an unexpected load added to her daily chores and responsibilities. Yet she couldn't say no to me the day I brought him home. But if he was to live with us, he had to obey the rules of the house. They weren't negotiable. Though in time, he'd learn to push her boundaries and she unwittingly yielded; her kindness and tolerance superseded all previous expectations.

All things considered, Sylvester was mostly a well-behaved cat. A firm command from us and he'd know he had crossed the line. "Don't jump on the bed," Mum would say to him. She didn't want his fur left all over the bedcovers. Particularly during moulting season, his fur would drop off in clumps. Removing it from the beds and carpet was a tedious and burdensome chore.

She'd be furious if he defied her by sitting on one of our beds. We all knew as soon as he did, no matter if it was for a brief moment, the bedspread would be besieged with clumps of fur.

So, the golden rule that we taught him as a kitten was that he was not to sit on the beds. We knew he understood, because we'd often see him stop in his tracks at the entrance of a bedroom, look at the bed, lick his lips—a tell-tale sign he was thinking about jumping on it—but wisely choosing not to. Then he'd walk away from the temptation. But sometimes his temptation won.

Sylvester grew into a sturdy yet agile cat. He'd climb, jump, and run with swiftness and prowess. He was energetic but also rebellious, and at times, he'd disobey the golden rule and jump onto the beds. Sometimes he'd go from one bed to another bed, from room to room. I think it was on purpose, just to upset my mum. He would select a bed dependent on the position of the sun and every time he'd get caught by my mum. She'd yell at him to get off it and then proceed to clean up the fur that was left behind on the bedspread. Many times we found him sleeping on the spare bed. He'd be positioned front and centre, with his front legs tucked under his torso and his head up, as if he were posing for a portrait. When he saw us enter through the door and cry out, "Sylvester! Get off the bed!" he'd casually awaken, look directly at us and blurt out an easy-going meow to acknowledge his wrongdoing. But we knew better; he didn't care. There was little veracity in him thinking he'd committed a transgression. Reluctantly, he'd jump off the bed and seek an alternative place to lie down; such as the top of the stairs or someplace where he'd not be disturbed.

The audacity of him. I guess from his perspective, it was 'we' who were annoying him and interrupting his sleep time, even though it was 'he' who had disregarded the golden rule. He couldn't care less about the fur he ditched from his coat, which created a trail of black and white cat hairs throughout the bedrooms. It would strew all over the bed quilts and scatter throughout the hallway, ending at the top of the staircase. Sylvester would, in the meantime, find a comfortable place of solitude and refuge from our squabbling voices.

Nonetheless, I loved him unconditionally. I'd cheekily laugh at his disobedience. My mother wouldn't be too thrilled by my lack of care. Logically speaking, I think a cat's manner is to be embraced. Their ability to live in the present and not act on past or future events is an enviable personality trait. I would appreciatively accept this trait into my daily life more readily if it were that simple. I believe we think too much about the past and the future at the expense of the present moment.

Cats are the most enlightened of creatures, with their ability to be playful and curious with their surroundings, and their ability to shrug off distress. That's a skill I wish I could readily access. Sylvester was no different to any other feline in that he had the ability to move on instantly from a negative experience. He'd carry on in play and merriment without having any reproach for the individual who'd moments earlier scolded him for slashing the lounge room sofa to bits with his sharpened claws.

4
The Ant Eats Sugar

I have a favourite place to sit in the morning; it's on top of the stairs. I gaze outside through a large glass window and watch the world around me. I see birds flying and leaves that rustle in the wind. Sometimes I see an ant or two. Today I notice one ant take a different path to the army of ants. I wonder where he's heading?

The sun is warm. It radiates through the glass window and blankets itself onto the stairway where I am lying. I feel the piercing sunrays as they touch my face and travel down my back and tail. The grass and trees are lime green in colour, with some shrubs bearing red fruit that feed the birds that sit on its branches. The air is freshly scented with newly cut grass. Yet with all the beauty that lies before me, it's the aroma of food that grabs my attention the most. The smell awakens my senses and my stomach. It's chicken for my lunchtime meal.

I love food so much I could eat all day long. Every time I smell food wafting through the air, my attention instantly turns toward the kitchen. As soon as my nostrils whiff the aroma, I dash down the stairs, race past the shoes lying in my path and reach the laundry where my food bowl awaits me. I bellow out an insistent meow, demanding they hurry up and place the succulent juicy pieces of chicken into my bowl. And someone is always compliant to my request to be served pronto. I've a readymade chef, waiter and cleaner at my beck and call. Oh, the luxury of being a cat.

"Your eyes are bigger than your stomach," Mum exclaims as she watches me gulp down the food. As I finish consuming the last of the chicken, I contemplate what scrumptious dish I'll be served for afternoon snack.

My food and water bowls have a constant supply of delicious food and fresh, clean water. I'm not too fussed about water; in fact, I'd rather not drink it. I'm not sure why they even bother filling the water bowl. It's always full to the brim whenever I have my meal served to me. I devour the food, but I leave the water untouched. Don't they understand that I don't intend to drink it? Sooner or later, they always succumb to my stubbornness and fill the water bowl with milk.

In my room lays my bed. It sits on an ironing board. To get into it, I take a giant leap up and onto the ironing board, landing confidently on all four legs. From there it's a small step or two into my cosy bed. I have blankets to keep me warm in the colder weather; and, when it's hot and humid, the window above the ironing board remains slightly ajar to allow the night breeze to soothe me. I notice in the warmer weather my fur coat gets too warm for me so I'm always grooming myself to remove excess fur, to the dislike of Mum. Every night as I fall asleep, the sound of the freezer softly buzzes. It sits adjacent to me and reminds me of my brother when he was asleep and purring away next to me.

I love my room and I love this house that's become my home. I'm glad to know I have a place of security. As the years pass, I grow into a mature cat. No more a mischievous kitten. I have muscular legs with a solid tummy; good food—being well looked after will do that to a cat. I'm physically strong and I walk with prowess throughout my domain. I'm king and I'm happy.

5

The Guru and the Balancing Scales

Sylvester was my animal guru; he enlightened me about how to live in peace and harmony in a world that's harsh and unrelenting. He had an innate ability to balance his emotional scales with every circumstance he encountered. My challenge was to do the same. Many a time I'd catch him staring at me and I'd sense he was conveying a message relevant for that moment.

On a wet and windy Wednesday during the depths of winter, I was having a calamity of a day. You know the type of day where as soon as you awaken everything goes wrong? It starts when you hit your toe on the bed leg, or maybe you miss the bus by 30 seconds. Or you spill your lunch all over your white shirt just before that important meeting. Well this day had been one of those days. Sylvester could see my frustration as soon as I arrived home from work. Normally he'd greet me as I entered, but not today. I must've been giving off a negative vibe. In his wisdom he respectfully gave me space.

After dinner, I went to sit in the lounge room to watch TV. In my mind I was still re-living the mishaps of the day. This was only making me feel more disgruntled and annoyed. Sylvester walked into the lounge room and sat directly in front of me, staring deeply into my eyes. I felt that was weird of him, so I watched him as he watched me. I sensed he was trying to communicate with me. I believe he was attempting to convey the message that I ought to align myself to my greater good. It was a feeling that's hard to explain. If it could be deciphered into words, he would have been saying: "Relax. The day is over. Wasteful energy is what you have, Ben."

I realised something powerful was happening in that moment. Sylvester was teaching me a universal wisdom so often seen in the animal kingdom and so often ignored by humans. His demeanour was an example to uphold. Calm and relaxed and consciously complete in the moment. I felt enlightened, and for the first time in a long time I heard his message. I took a deep breath and counted one, two three... He continued to stare at me. His pose was symbolic: paws perfectly placed next to each other, tail swept around his body. He resembled a Tibetan monk in a transcendental state of meditation.

I exhaled and placed my attention on the now. Just like him. I glanced up at the TV; the movie was about to start. I looked back at Sylvester, he'd moved on to someplace else in the house. The Zen master had completed the lesson.

Sylvester had the ability to refocus his attention away from a moment that didn't please him. He'd switch off mentally, placing his attention on the trees rustling in the wind or the sound of the cars in the neighbourhood street passing by, or the smell of food in the kitchen. He didn't worry about the unpleasant moment that had just passed. Unlike humans, he didn't hold resentment or anger, or even feel sorry for himself. He just moved on. It was an invaluable lesson for me to learn. The beauty of animals is their ability to shrug things off just as quickly as a light switching off.

He also had extraordinary senses, ethereal to say the least. In many instances he'd anticipate hiding even before he'd heard the clinking and rattling of the cat carrier.

Almost always he'd be behind the couch or inside my wardrobe well before we'd made our way to the cellar to pick up the cat carrier. Even more astonishing as he became wiser in his old age, was his seeming ability to read our thoughts.

I recall a day we had booked him to see the local vet for a 2:30pm appointment. At 2:10pm I was about to mention to Mum that it was time to grab the cat carrier from under the cellar. But before I'd spoken one word, Sylvester, who had been sitting next to me, dashed upstairs and hid under my bed.

We couldn't believe what we had just witnessed and were dumbfounded as to how he had known what we were thinking. It was as if he'd read our minds and pre-empted our next move.

He'd let me know when Mum was about to drive into the driveway. Well before she actually did so, he'd be sitting at the front door awaiting her arrival. My summation was he either had extraordinary hearing or he was spiritually in-tune. If he could hear the sound of cars from a distance, how did he know the sound was the sound of Mum's car? And if he was spiritually in-tune… well I can't explain that. What I did know for sure was that he was something special.

With the passage of time and the benefit of hindsight, a flood of memories like the examples above cross my mind. All of which speak of the same theme, that Sylvester had a sixth sense and a natural ability to shift focus instantly.

Equally it didn't matter to him where he sat as long as he was comfortable. Many a time it was in the most nonsensical of places: the top of a shelf in between some dusty books, inside a cupboard or even in the shower, it didn't matter to him. I'd look at him and he'd gaze back with his big green eyes bestow a meow, readjust his paws that were tucked under his body, and then nod off to sleep. He chose to live each moment as each moment arrived. It's a quality cats have; to not worry about the future or feel guilty about the past. They just accept the moment and do what pleases them, even if it's to sleep on the top of the freezer or some other ungodly place that only a cat could appreciate.

He didn't have to sit down and counsel me, reason with me, or question me. He just had to be himself. He was a set of scales that tipped back and forth with ease to find equilibrium. He did so by doing the simple things; never trying to impress, and never feeling down and out. It was his endearing feline traits that kept me enchanted every day. As the years passed, he never changed. He was like a rock in the ocean that would sit and allow the ocean waves to sweep across it; he was just as resilient and unwavering. He was always steadfast and predictable, regardless of the circumstances of the day. I loved that about him.

He'd brighten my mood in an instant. He'd walk into a room, get my attention and then head to the nearest mat or couch, to let everyone know he'd moved on from the previous five minutes. He didn't care, he wouldn't mull over something, and he wouldn't mind if he was told not to scratch the couch or be yelled at for leaving a trail of fur that created a mess on the carpet. To him it was wasted energy.

Sylvester was my guru, my master of emotional learning. I'd always fall short in understanding the lesson provided by him. I can't help but think the simple things in life are often the best; the finest days are the simple ones. Yet I was forever trapped in a conundrum of striving and never arriving to a blissful state of being. A friend like Sylvester always kept things real. I was thankful that he was around me to teach me (a lesson I'm still mastering) to stay level-headed in the turbulent waves of life that would inevitably come my way.

"I have lived with several Zen Masters, all of them cats."
Eckhart Tolle

6

The Wise Ol' Owl

I see the sliding door is open and stick my nose out to see how far I can venture outside before Ben or Mum catches me.

No one is around. My heart starts pounding as I make my way through the garden bed, sniffing and exploring around the roots of the shrubs. What's over there?

I decide to take a few more steps into unfamiliar territory. I've never been this far outside without Ben and Mum by my side. I'm nervous but excited at the same time. My legs tremble and I feel like I need to go use my kitty litter. I look into the distance and see a bird perched on a small tree. Instinctively, I crouch down low, tail swiping vigorously. I'm ready to attack my prey. But it flies away. I look the other way and there's a bee buzzing over a flower. I smell the air as the scent of the flower blows my way. The floral scent stimulates my senses and momentarily my nerves are soothed. I ignore the bee and head towards the back of the garden. There's a heap of wood planks lying in a corner of the garden bed. Like any curious cat, I stroll over to investigate. I climb to the top of the heap of wood and leap up onto the fence that divides my backyard from the neighbour's garden. I perch myself upon it. The view is surreal. My

FOREVER PURRFECT

heart skips a beat, not because of the potential danger, but in anticipation of the adventure that awaits. There's still no sign of Ben or Mum.

I jump down and land on freshly mowed lawn. Three tall eucalyptus trees stand like skyscrapers, freshly laid topsoil is strewn throughout the rose garden beds. Startled by a sound, I turn around and see water gushing out of a tap. It must have been left on accidentally by the neighbour. Cautiously I walk over to inspect it. I look up and see an ugly brute of a dog staring at me. He'd been sitting on the porch and must have seen me walking across his turf. He barks ferociously. Terrified, I dash at top speed down an alleyway and up a tree. I take a moment to catch my breath. When at last the dog has given up looking for me, I dismount and continue my walk along a pebbled path. I'm feeling a little fatigued, but my sense of adventure pushes me to walk some more. I walk for some time only to realise I've lost my way. I start to panic, as I can't recall how to get back home. I'm never going to see my family again.

In the distance I see a bird sitting in a tree; it's a wise looking bird. He's beige in colour and has two big brown eyes. He calls me over with a hoot and asks if I'm lost. I say yes, I am.

He turns to me and says, "If I were you, I'd look to the ground and follow your paw prints." I thank him for his wise words. I look down at the ground and he's right. My paws have left distinct impressions in the soft ground. Looking behind me I can see a trail leading away from the tree, back the way I came.

I begin my journey back home. My eyes dart back and forth, scanning, scanning. I'm certain I'll encounter another dog around each corner. Or worse...

Another cat! Up ahead, a scruffy-looking alley cat who, by the looks of it, hasn't had a good feed in months. I try not to get its attention as I sniff the air searching for the familiar scent of home.

"Hello," it says.

Oh no, I think to myself as it walks towards me.

"What brings you to my neighbourhood?"

"Umm... I was just on my way home from visiting a friend," I say uneasily.

The alley cat walks towards me and begins to smell me. It then bellows out a hideous howl that scares the living daylights out of me.

I turn and run as fast as I have ever run before. Up the street to the left and then to the right I go. I run and run, not daring to look behind me, hoping the alley cat is no longer chasing me. With a rush of adrenaline pumping through my veins, I leap onto a car that's parked on the side of the street. I take a few deep breaths to calm myself down, my heart still beating frantically. Looking over my shoulder, I don't see the cat. I swallow and lick my dry lips. I'm glad my unexpected encounter with the alley cat didn't end up in a street fight.

A fresh breeze blows in my direction. I lift my nose and smell the array of scents that travel with the wind. I smell home. I jump off the car onto the asphalt and head towards the smell of freshly-cooked schnitzel and fried potatoes.

I've walked about twenty metres down the road when I start to recognise my surroundings. I'm comforted to see the eucalyptus trees, the tap with the water still gushing from it, and the ugly brute of a dog. Thankfully, it's now fast asleep on the neighbour's back porch. Walking stealthily, so as not to wake it, I approach the fence. I take a deep breath and leap onto it. I see the backyard of my home. I jump, landing on a small shrub, my hind leg momentarily caught in the shrub branches. With an almighty kick, I escape its clutches. A few shakes of my leg and I shed the bug that had jumped onto me from the leaves. I continue to walk through the tomato plants, past the fig tree and finally dart through the side door, which is still open.

As I walk in, I see Mum in the laundry. "Sylvester, where have you been? You're covered in dirt and cobwebs."

I lick my lips and sheepishly walk to my bed. She picks me up and cleans me before placing me back in my bed. I take a deep breath and my heart finally stops racing.

Well, wasn't that a fun adventure?

7

When It Rains It Pours

As a kitten, Sylvester seldom had a health problem, with the exception of periodontal disease, caused by a build-up of plaque on his upper left side premolars. He'd chew food predominately with his upper and lower right-side premolars and molars. It was visually evident to see because his head tilted right to compensate chewing with his left side teeth. It was nothing to be overly concerned about. Just something to be mindful of.

In the spring of 2013, Sylvester's health changed for the worse. He was fourteen years old in human years or seventy-two in cat years.

It was a Thursday afternoon in late September; Mum called me to say she found blood in Sylvester's kitty litter but he appeared to be okay. To be sure it wasn't anything sinister, we booked in a time to see the local vet. It was scheduled for the following day. The next morning Sylvester was very quiet. He remained in his bed for most of the morning sleeping for the best part of it.

Our local vet had attended to Sylvester since we had adopted him. She'd see him for general health and dental check-ups. The visits were always an upheaval for Sylvester; he'd meow in despair when we'd take him to the vet clinic. His constant meowing was like hearing an annoying song on repeat. The vet clinic was easy to get to, situated in a local shopping strip. It had an unassuming frontage. Upon entering, a bell would signal our arrival. The reception and waiting area was welcoming; however, it was a sterile environment, one you'd expect from a vet clinic. The walls and ceiling were painted white and adorned with pictures of animals. Upon setting foot inside, you'd smell disinfectant and the odd odour wafting towards you from a canine sitting with its owner in the waiting room. All dressed in white coats, the staff and veterinarians were polite and understanding. Their love for animals was evident. They always gave me a sense of confidence that all would be okay with Sylvester when we took him in for a check-up. But from this day forward we'd be seeing a lot more of them.

We took Sylvester to the local vet clinic around mid-afternoon. His vet checked him over and ran some tests to confirm that he was bleeding internally.

Packed cell volume (PCV), also called hematocrit, is a measure of the percentage of red blood cells in the total blood volume. A normal range of PCV for cats is between 30–45%. Cats that have a value below 25% PCV are anaemic. Abnormal PCV values can also indicate dehydration, kidney disease or feline leukaemia. Physical signs are a pale nose, gums and paw pads.

Sylvester's PCV was at 15%, a dangerously low level. The vet wasn't able to establish why he was losing blood at such a quick rate, so she immediately referred him to a specialist vet. Thankfully the veterinary specialist centre could see Sylvester right away. It was a ten-minute drive, so we set off immediately with Sylvester huddled on Mum's lap in the back seat and me driving. Glancing in the rear-view mirror, I could see Sylvester in the back seat with Mum. He looked exhausted. I caught my reflection in the mirror; my eyes looked heavy and my complexion was a pale white. Fear was consuming me.

When we walked into the specialist centre, the receptionist directed us to a consulting room. The specialist vet saw to Sylvester in a matter of minutes. They did another PCV test. The results showed his PCV had dropped since his last test less than half an hour ago. It was at 10%. The vet concluded that with the rapidly declining PCV levels, Sylvester was heading into shock. His organs would begin to shut down if untreated. He required an immediate blood transfusion.

The specialist vet couldn't perform a blood transfusion at the centre as there was no available donor cat that had Sylvester's blood type. The specialist vet contacted multiple veterinary clinics around town to find an available match. Fortunately she found a 24-hour emergency vet clinic with a donor cat that had a blood type matching Sylvester's; however the emergency clinic was on the other side of the city, an hour or so travel time. It was also peak hour traffic, made even busier than usual by the heightened activity in the city surrounding the Australian Rules Grand Final on the following afternoon. To add to our challenging dilemma, there was no medical transportation available, so to get Sylvester there, we had to drive him ourselves. If we didn't make the drive, he would certainly pass away by evening.

I mustered up the strength and said to Mum, "We can make it." So we set off to drive through the city in peak hour traffic. It was a race against the clock. I had to remain composed, strong and vigilant, even though I was at breaking point emotionally. I prayed and prayed relentlessly throughout the travel, believing within my heart that he'd be okay.

Peak hour traffic didn't help. Cars and trucks making their way home were squashed like sardines in a tin can along the busy roads. I needed to stay calm and patient; but annoyingly, as we approached every intersection, the traffic lights turned red. It's as if they knew our predicament and wickedly remained red to distress us further. We were gridlocked once we entered the city. We were fighting the fight, moment by moment, whilst our nemesis time ticked over and over again. Any advantage like a green light was a godsend.

Stuck at the red light, I twisted around to check on Sylvester. He was motionless, sitting on Mum's lap. His nose was no longer pink but an opaque white, his glassy eyes were staring directly in front of him as if they were glued in that position. There was no acknowledgement from him when I called his name. Turning back to focus on the traffic, I summoned my will to keep on going, even though deep down inside I was petrified. I couldn't allow myself to fall into a downward spiral of negativity, so I refocused on the road ahead. I took a few deep breaths and calmed myself down. Just as Sylvester my Zen master had taught me.

An hour or so later we arrived at the emergency vet clinic. Sylvester was required to stay overnight to receive the blood transfusion. My heart sank at the thought of leaving him overnight, but it had to be if he was to have any chance of survival.

I kissed him on his head goodnight and left the room quickly. I didn't turn back to see him one more time in case it was the last time. Not today. I wouldn't get worked up and cry because of fearful thoughts and gloom.

That evening for me was horrendous; sleep was near impossible. Fearful thoughts continuously raced through my mind, sprinkled infrequently with optimistic ones. Throughout my sleepless night, my attention was stuck on the sound of the clock. The consistent tick was a security blanket. It kept me anchored and gave me comfort. The more it ticked over, the closer it was to the time I'd get up and travel to the only thing that mattered to me right then, Sylvester.

At the first break of daylight, I was up and out of bed. Turning on the TV, I saw the main news story was the Grand Final that was happening today. Normally I'd be engrossed in watching the national sporting event but today I wasn't interested. My attention was on the mid-morning traffic around the city as it was beginning to become congested with enthusiasts and followers of the sport making their way to the ground for the 2:30 pm start of the game. My mind was planning ahead to the quickest route to travel to get to Sylvester sooner, knowing full well it was a lengthy drive to the emergency clinic even without the unusual traffic build up. There was also no way around the city to get to the emergency clinic. I refocused my thoughts to making the call to the clinic. My heart was beating incredibly fast as the phone connected. After a few rings, the receptionist answered. I asked her how Sylvester was doing.

She paused for a moment and then said, "He is doing okay. His vitals have stabilized and his PCV is up to a good level. He's out of the danger zone, for the time being."

"Can we come pick him up?"

"Yes, you can. Say in the next hour or so? We're getting him to eat some food so hopefully he does eat something before you get here," she said.

Mum and I were both relieved. The blood transfusion had gone well and he was able to come home. After hanging up the phone, I paused to gather my thoughts, take a deep breath and realign myself. He was okay.

8

The Final Siren Sounds

The trip to the emergency vet clinic was less stressful this time round but doubts about Sylvester's condition crossed my mind multiple times. Each time I felt my stomach sink. At least the roads were unobstructed, unlike the afternoon before. Maybe luck would be on our side today.

Arriving a lot faster than expected, some forty minutes later, Mum and I headed into the emergency clinic and made our way to reception. The attending nurse had already prepared Sylvester for his trip home. Seeing him come out from the consulting room was a massive relief. The most negative thoughts of Sylvester not making it through the night, which had plagued my mind, hadn't come true. We'd had a small victory but there was still a fight ahead of us. Up until now step by step had been my mantra; and with each footstep I edged closer to salvation. So I'd continue with this formula. The current step we'd negotiated successfully, now onto the next...

This was the second time I'd felt an immense fear of losing Sylvester. I remember the first so clearly. It was a lazy Sunday afternoon, and I was out to lunch with a friend at a local cafe when I received a call from Mum saying she couldn't find Sylvester. It had only been a few weeks since we had adopted him and naturally, I was very protective of him. I'd recently lost a pet to a road incident and the dread of it happening again was overwhelming.

I dashed home to begin searching for him. My first thought was to check if he'd snuck outside. We looked high and low, but we couldn't find him. I couldn't believe he was gone. I began to trace the likely steps he'd have made before disappearing. There was some doubt as to whether he'd escaped outside, so we redirected the search inside the house. Frantic thoughts raced through my mind: what if he was trapped somewhere and unable to meow loud enough for us to hear him? Suddenly, I had a thought: did someone ring the doorbell? I instantly checked behind the sofas in the lounge room—that was the place we'd found him when the doorbell had rung on other occasions. I guess the narrow space between the wall and the sofa felt like a safe haven for him. There were eight single-seater sofas in total. One by one, I pulled the sofas away from the wall; one by one, Sylvester wasn't there. As I pulled the last sofa away, I looked over the arm rest to the underside of its belly; Sylvester was quietly sitting there. He looked up at me with a guilty gaze in his gleaming green eyes that professed, "Here I am!"

If only my fear could be dispelled as easily this time. Before we had left the emergency clinic to take Sylvester home, the attending vet had informed us that his PCV levels would fall to dangerous levels again if the root cause of the bleeding was not diagnosed and treated. Having tested him prior to us arriving they'd already started to decline so time was of the essence to find out why he was bleeding internally. Only the specialist vets could help him now.

So instead of heading home we took him straight back to the veterinary specialist centre for the vet to attend to him. Thankfully a vet specialising in digestive diseases was available. The receptionist booked a time for Sylvester to be seen as soon as we'd arrive. Forty minutes later we reached the centre. Sylvester looked like he had the day before. He was very quiet and his nose, paws and gums were getting paler by the minute; a tell-tale sign he was verging on anaemic.

We sat in the waiting room full of pets and their concerned owners. The day was cool and so too was the room. It was a bigger clinic than our local vet, with numerous consulting rooms surrounding the waiting area. I tentatively picked up a magazine from the stand next to where I was sitting. Sylvester was resting beside me in his cat carrier. A border collie came our way and sat adjacent to me, right next to the water bowl on offer to the visiting animals. As I flicked through the magazine, I was not surprised to see it was outdated. I skimmed through the pages, trying to focus my attention on the celebrity scandals strewn over them, but my mind kept veering to the uncertainty at hand.

We were called into the consulting room by the attending specialist vet. After checking Sylvester's reports, the vet concluded that, without performing a colonoscopy, he'd just be guessing at the cause and treatment of the excessive internal bleeding. The blood in Sylvester's stool was dark red, an indication the bleeding stemmed from the upper intestine. But without seeing internally, that couldn't be known for certain. We concluded Sylvester had to have a colonoscopy.

We headed home, leaving Sylvester to have the procedure. Like the night before, we were waiting anxiously back at home for the results. My negative thoughts started again, interjecting and standing over any positive thoughts that I struggled to muster up. In my mind I was in combat against pessimism.

Time passed slowly that mid-morning.

While I was making a toasted sandwich, filled with my favourite leftover food from the night before, my phone rang. It was the specialist vet calling to inform me Sylvester's PCV had rapidly dropped down to a life-threatening level. He didn't want to risk putting Sylvester under anaesthetic; with his age of fourteen years and the internal bleeding, the danger was too high. We agreed to not proceed with the colonoscopy.

Sylvester's PCV had now dropped to 4%. Very little could be done for him.

Shocked, in despair, and feeling numb all over, I couldn't accept this was the end for him. I just knew he'd be okay, I had a strong feeling he'd get through this. To this day, I can't explain why I felt that way, but I did. Whether I was in denial or not, my attention was solely focused on helping Sylvester recover. I felt calm and determined. I'd help Sylvester recover and he'd be okay.

The specialist vet said the options available were to euthanise him or to take him home to pass away. I chose to bring him home. I was distraught and in tears but I still had hope.

My attention for the next couple of hours was solely on Sylvester. I didn't leave his side. I wanted to nurse him back to good health; I was ignoring the opinions of others that he was going to die. I remained positive every second of every minute of every hour. I was by his side throughout the evening. I didn't want to leave him alone. Throughout the night, he'd wearyingly glance over at me to acknowledge my presence. I believed he was grateful that I was there to watch over him. He'd then nod off to sleep. I could hear his heart beating, his chest moving up and down, breathing in the essential air that gave him life. At times when I patted him, he'd purr harmoniously. The sound was music to my ears. He was comfortable and at peace. It was a perfect environment for his natural healing process to take over and sanction an overhaul of the ravages that were taking place in his intestines.

Before we had left the veterinary specialist centre that morning, the vet had given us one small window of hope; he had prescribed an antacid tablet to be taken once a day in the hope of lowering the acid levels in Sylvester's digestive tract. Once that was under control, his body could naturally heal itself. It was assumed (without being able to do a colonoscopy to see his digestive tract) that his digestive lining was ulcerated and that was why there was an enormous amount of internal bleeding. The antacid was our last chance to save him.

Many people thought Sylvester would pass away that weekend.

He didn't die. He lived.

Miraculously, his health improved. In the following days, he was able to get up from his bed and take short walks through the house. His insatiable desire for food returned. Day after day, he regained his vitality and strength.

We were observing a miracle right before our eyes.

In the following days, weeks and months, we were scrupulous in caring for him. He ate only the highest quality food, specially created to assist in feline digestive disorders, he drank the purest spring water and he slumbered in the comfort of a different bed in each of his favourite places around the house. One bed we placed on the top of the stairs next to the window, another in the lounge room adjacent to where Mum sat in the evenings and, of course, one in his bedroom, now placed on the ground and not on the ironing board. We weren't taking any chances of him accidently misjudging his dismount from his bed to the floor. Any slight health concern sent us back to the local vet immediately.

I was very grateful that he had a second chance at life; to see him walk again and for him to watch in wonder from the upstairs window the sights and sounds of the birds and insects amidst the warmth of the sunshine as it shone upon his face. As I walked past him one morning, it appeared to me that he was deep in thought, almost as though he was recalling the events of the last couple of weeks.

9

Raining Cats and More Cats

I don't feel well.

"What's wrong Sylvester," says Mum.

I lay in my bed with my front paws wrapped over my head, huddled in between the blankets I hear birds chirping, but this morning I'm not up to watching them.

Ben picks me up, my body limp as he cradles me. He gently pats me on the head as he places me into the cat carrier. The cat carrier can mean only one thing; I'm visiting the place for sick animals, a place where humans who care for animals wear white coats. I've been in the cat carrier many times before; I have never liked it, not because it's uncomfortable to sit in, but because I know where it's taking me.

In the waiting room, I notice a cat and a dog sitting with their human friends. The cat is attempting to sleep whilst the miniature white dog yaps away. As is most often the case, the dog is more inquisitive than the cat. It snoops around the room not minding its own business. I wish it would sit down and behave.

When I come here, a familiar face sees to me. She's caring and looks after me. Today she checks my mouth and feels my tummy. It's uncomfortable when she examines me and I meow to tell her that it hurts.

I sigh. I'm feeling very unwell. Ben places me into the cat carrier. I sense something isn't right by the look on everyone's faces; Ben and Mum seem worried. I'm feeling exhausted, no strength to meow. I swallow incessantly to moisten my throat; a habit of mine when I'm facing uncertainty.

We travel to a place that has other sick cats and dogs. I've never visited this place before. I'm anxious for what is in store for me. I'm seen to by a lady who examines me and chats at great length with Ben and Mum. I'm scared, not to mention my stomach feels like it's on fire. I'm momentarily out of the cat carrier and free to walk around the room. As they continue to speak to one another, I find comfort and safety jumping onto Ben's lap. He holds me tight and pats me. He looks worried and dismayed at the conversation taking place.

After their conversation, I'm once again placed into the cat carrier and we head off; I'm hoping we're heading home. The sun is setting; the sky is sapphire blue with an orange tinge from the dimming sunlight, swathed with hazy white smoke whispered clouds. I'm sitting in the back seat of the car; Mum is holding me. I sense we're heading someplace other than home. Right now, I'm too weary to care.

The car stops and I'm taken inside another unfamiliar place. It looks similar to the place I've just come from with similar smells. I see a couple of cats and a rabbit sitting in the corner of the room; like me it's in a cat carrier. Its ears protrude out from the confines of the steel bars. Unexpectedly, Ben and Mum say goodbye to me and leave me with a young woman wearing a white coat. I'm petrified. Where am I? Why did Ben and Mum leave me here?

The young woman sticks a sharp needle into my front leg. Ouch! She pats me reassuringly. I feel like I've been stung by a bee. Those pesky bees. I never cared to chase them in the garden.

I'm in a room with three cats. They don't seem happy. One, in particular, doesn't look well; the other two are frightened and stressed. I'm tired and I need to rest so I close my eyes and doze off to sleep.

I awaken to the sounds of Ben and Mum's voices. I hear them in the next room. I scan my surroundings and I see two cats sitting adjacent to me. The unwell cat is no longer present. I wonder what happened to him?

I'm feeling better today. I stretch my legs as I take a yawn.

The lady places me into the cat carrier and brings me out to where Ben and Mum are anxiously waiting. I'm happy to see them, but they look troubled and very tired. I hope they've come to take me home. Moments later, I'm back in the car; I hope it's not a long drive home.

I sense something isn't right. I realise we're not heading home but back to the other place we visited yesterday. I think for a moment about my warm cosy bed and how I want to be sleeping in it right now. I want it more than I want to eat food. Come to think of it, I'm not feeling hungry today.

Entering the building, there's the familiar smell of detergent masking the odours of sick dogs, cats, birds and other animals. I'm confused as to why I'm here again. The humans in the white coats are around me, endlessly checking over me. The man in the white coat is pressing gently on my stomach. I feel pain all over. What did I eat? Was it that cockroach I captured the other day? I should be careful not to eat dirty insects.

Once again, I'm placed into the cat carrier; it's become my second home. I look up at Ben as he gazes back at me, "It's okay, Sylvester. We're going home now." He looks incredibly sad. I've never seen him so sad. He repeats, "Everything is going to be okay."

I'm not sure why he looks so incredibly sad. I see it in his eyes. I'm worried about him.

Arriving back home, I'm lifted out of the cat carrier and placed delicately into my bed. I'm wrapped up in my blanket. It's nice and warm. Hours pass and Ben has not left my side. He continues to talk to me and pat me oh-so-gently and cautiously. I start purring to reassure him I'm okay. But honestly, I'm extremely worn-out. I go to sleep.

Over the next couple of days I feel increasingly better. I've gained some strength and I'm feeling a tad more energetic. I nibble on a couple of dry food pellets. The burning sensation remains in my stomach; especially after I've eaten, so I decide its best not to eat too much food. Ben is still worried but not as sad as he was the other day. I see a smile or two from him as he continues to talk to me. I look at him and acknowledge with a purr and a meow that I will be okay. As soon as I'm feeling better, I promise myself, I'll play ball with him.

A few days pass and I'm feeling a whole lot better. I have strength in my legs to walk around and to climb to the top of the stairs. I peer out the window and see nature at its finest. The birds are chirping, and the sun is shining. The days are warmer, and the daylight is staying around longer. I smell the soft breeze overtly scented with freshly cut grass and the blooming yellow flowers, as the wind carries their scent towards my nose. I take a breath of the fresh air. I look down at the ground and I see the ants marching once again. I fixate on one ant as it takes off in another direction. I wonder where he's going?

10
Scraps of Paper

Sunrise and I'm awoken by the birds chirping outside my window. Mum opens the door to my room and heads to my food bowl. She has my breakfast in hand. With eyes still half closed, I jump out of my bed and leap towards the food bowl before she's had a chance to serve it.

Yum, it's turkey. The aroma wafts up my nose as she scoops the pieces out of the tin.

"Wait, Sylvester!" she exclaims. I can't wait; I'm starving! "Give me a chance to get the food out of the tin," she shouts at me.

I take a step back, my eyes transfixed on the pieces of meat that tumble out of the tin and into my bowl.

No, I can't wait. I gulp down the first pieces of turkey.

"Sylvester, slow down and chew your food," she says. I ignore her and carry on gulping down the remaining pieces of turkey. "And drink some water," she insists.

I respond kindly with a meow, "No thanks, I only want food."

After my feed and with a full belly, I waddle to my bed and sluggishly get into it. I proceed to clean myself, as I always do after eating, cleaning my face with my paws and licking my lips relentlessly.

I sometimes hear Ben say to me with a chuckle, "Sylvester, why do you lick your lips so much after you eat?"

It's a cat's obsession to be clean. It's a natural part of being a cat. Along with my brothers and sister, I learned from birth to impeccably clean myself. I wonder where my siblings are now? I hope they're happy and living in nice homes with loving families. I miss them.

My tummy is bloated full to the brim. I must be careful not to upset my stomach. I don't want to go through the pain I went through last time. I must listen to Ben and Mum when they tell me to slow down when eating; chew more and then swallow, don't just swallow. But I can't resist wolfing down my food. I don't care what food it is, chicken, beef, lamb or tuna, I will devour it.

The most blissful part of my day is early evening when Mum sits down to relax in the lounge room. I jump on her lap where it's warm and comfortable. I purr as I get myself snug and doze off to sleep. She lets me sit on her lap every night. I feel safe and loved.

Lately though, I don't feel like I once did. Years ago, I'd run up and down the hallway, full of energy, chasing flies that snuck through the front door or frolicking with scraps of paper that happened to be accidently dropped on the floor. Nowadays I ignore the flies and the scraps of paper. I simply don't care, and I can't be bothered to waste my energy on needless things.

I often hear Mum say to me, "You old puss." Perhaps she notices my desire to sleep all day, eat when hungry and to do nothing more. Or maybe she has noticed some grey whiskers adorning my cheeks and eyebrows. I believe they make me look distinguished.

Truth be told, I'm feeling old. I feel it in my limbs. I've noticed my legs look wirier and less muscular. My fur isn't as robust as it once was, and the colour looks slightly dull. The shine is still there but not as intense. The skin around my stomach has drooped and it hangs unattractively like an ill-fitting garment. My eyes aren't working as they used to; I mistake crumbs on the floor for insects. Despite my body wearingly aging, my hearing remains acute. My ears pivot to the direction of noise like antennae picking up the frequency of sound.

I take a deep breath and exhale a lament. I must get some sleep.

11

Empty Sterile Corridors

Sylvester's health was my number one priority in the ensuing days, weeks and months. Unfortunately, he'd never have the same good bill of health that he'd once had so we were always on alert if he suddenly felt unwell.

For that reason, I wanted a greater understanding of his illness. The knowledge sustained me emotionally, giving me the feeling of control in an uncontrollable situation. Any uncharacteristic behaviour in Sylvester signalled to me the start of a potential flare-up of his condition. As I'd learned previously, time was of the essence in treating him.

Without Sylvester having a colonoscopy, we were only managing his condition. But the colonoscopy was too risky, and the fact that he was functioning as close as possible to a healthy cat's life was enough to be content with at the present moment.

The ambiguity of Sylvester's gastric illness meant we were on call 24/7 to deal with an impending emergency. Eventually the emergencies were no longer unexpected, they were all too regular; a stomach spasm, general malaise, or a presentation of unusual temperament called for us to pause our lives and direct our attention to seeking medical assistance. It was emotionally draining.

I'll never forget one late winter's evening when the unexpected happened to him. It was bedtime for Sylvester. His usual routine was he'd eat some food and then jump into his bed. Like clockwork, he'd commence his nightly ritual, kneading his blanket and purring. Within a few minutes, his eyelids would become top heavy and he'd fall asleep.

This particular evening, Sylvester's routine didn't go as scheduled; after eating his dinner and jumping into bed, he started to shake uncontrollably from paw to tail. It looked like he was having a seizure. I was absolutely horrified. He hopped out of his bed and vomited, expelling the food he had just consumed onto the laundry floor. He then walked out of the laundry room and started to pace up and down the hallway. I'd never seen this type of behaviour from him. My anxiety went through the roof; my heart pounding, a wave of fear came over me. It was clear to me something wasn't right with him. He continued to act peculiar: walking a few steps, then stopping in his tracks, staring at the ground and starting to walk again. This happened over and over again. Although I was scared, I had become accustomed to expecting the unexpected with him. The suddenness of a behavioural change wasn't a shock anymore, but just an indicator to respond quickly and take necessary actions.

I rushed him to the 24-hour emergency veterinary clinic.

Sylvester was one of two animals waiting to be seen by an attending vet. It was past midnight and freezing cold. Although anxious, tired and weary, I remained stoic amid the challenging situation. Although unwelcome thoughts did cross my mind, I stayed rational and positive. "It's just another episode he's going through. All will be okay," I kept saying to myself. But then I'd think, am I kidding myself?

I kept recalling that September afternoon almost two years ago when he'd almost died.

I took a deep breath to recompose myself. I looked up at the noticeboard on the wall. It was plastered with information on animals that visited the clinic. Distraction was my friend now. I kept looking at Sylvester. He was lying motionless in his basket but I could gain his attention by waving my index finger through the cat carrier in front of his nose. Normally, he'd take a half-hearted bite at it but this time there was no reaction from him. He seemed dazed, only distracted by the large, muscular dog sitting opposite us with its owner.

Again, my mind went off on a tangent. Will his luck run out tonight? Will he die? Just as quickly as the thought entered my mind, I kicked it out. I refocused my attention on the front counter, hoping the attendant was about to call Sylvester's name so we could go into the consulting rooms. But it didn't happen; they were busy attending to paperwork unrelated to Sylvester. I tried sending out vibes to them, "Call his name, call it now!" But that didn't work.

I sighed and closed my eyes momentarily, trying to trick myself that I'd just awoken from a deep sleep. I wasn't fooled. I was feeling too tired and irritable. I wished

I could ask Sylvester how he was doing. I was sure he was wondering why he was here at this ungodly hour. I wondered if this moment brought back memories for him of the night we had left him at the emergency veterinary clinic to get a blood transfusion. I wondered if he was upset with me or sad for me, that I'm going through this once again with him.

I'll never know what he was thinking or feeling or whether in his cat's mind he could feel sadness. I contemplated if he understood it was not just him, but both of us, suffering. I'd never know.

I fantasised momentarily: if he could speak to me whilst we both waited, perhaps he'd say, "I'm okay, Ben. Just feeling a little queasy." Hearing that from him would have alleviated so much of the anxiety that was consuming me at that moment.

Another thought crossed my mind: I have work in the morning and it's now 2am.

We spent the next couple of hours in the waiting room. Considering they weren't busy, I couldn't understand why it was taking so long for him to be seen. I became more and more frustrated as the minutes ticked by.

"Sylvester," the attendant finally shouted from the front counter they'd been sitting at most of the evening. The sound of his name bellowed down the white sterile corridor towards our ears. At last, it was his turn to be seen. He was assessed by the attending vet. I remained focused and calm, allowing the vet to do his job. I educated the vet of Sylvester's entire medical history succinctly, so as not to waste another moment. The vet checked Sylvester over. He concluded the likely cause of Sylvester's sudden downturn was digestive malaise. He prescribed some medication to make Sylvester feel at ease. From his assessment, the vet said there wasn't enough evidence to draw a conclusive diagnosis; Sylvester may have had pains in the stomach, he may have been startled or he may have been anxious. Either way, the vet wasn't sure what had caused him to act strangely and vomit. Sylvester was okay to go home.

It was a stressful night. It was very late and I was tired and drained but thankful Sylvester was okay for now. We were none-the-wiser as to why he had become unwell during the evening. The sacrifice I made for him that night, like the many before and the many that would follow, paled in significance next to Sylvester's health.

On that evening and the many more like it that followed, I learned important lessons: to be resolute and resilient when faced with a difficult situation, to maintain a positive frame of mind when making decisions, and to filter negative thoughts in times of stress. It was the combination of these virtues that steered me through challenging times with Sylvester.

Sylvester was always a brave cat in these situations; trusting in us to do what was best for him. The obstacles he faced made me feel sad that he had to endure this frequent provocation to his health. This disease, disorder, or whatever was invading him, was a disruption to his life. It was unfair and it was unsympathetic when it stuck its ugly head up. Yet it allowed me to become resolute in defeating it, for it wasn't going to overwhelm me, nor Sylvester, certainly not on my watch.

Sylvester was my inspiration to never give up and to keep going when things seemed dire and defeat beckoned. I'd be taken aback by his self-control. Like the times we sat together in the passenger's seat of the car on our way to see the vet. Sylvester would be preoccupied by the outside surroundings as he peered out the car window. His bulbous green eyes would dart around, up and down, side to side, as he watched the cars travelling by and the overhanging curbside trees with their wiry branches that waved at him as we passed by. In those moments, I thought distraction was his way of dealing with uncertainty. But I think differently now. He just placed his attention on good things, things that weren't a threat, that didn't hurt him or act unkind to him. Pure bliss was his mantra. In time I'd come to terms with the fact that Sylvester outshone me when the going got tough. But that was okay by me.

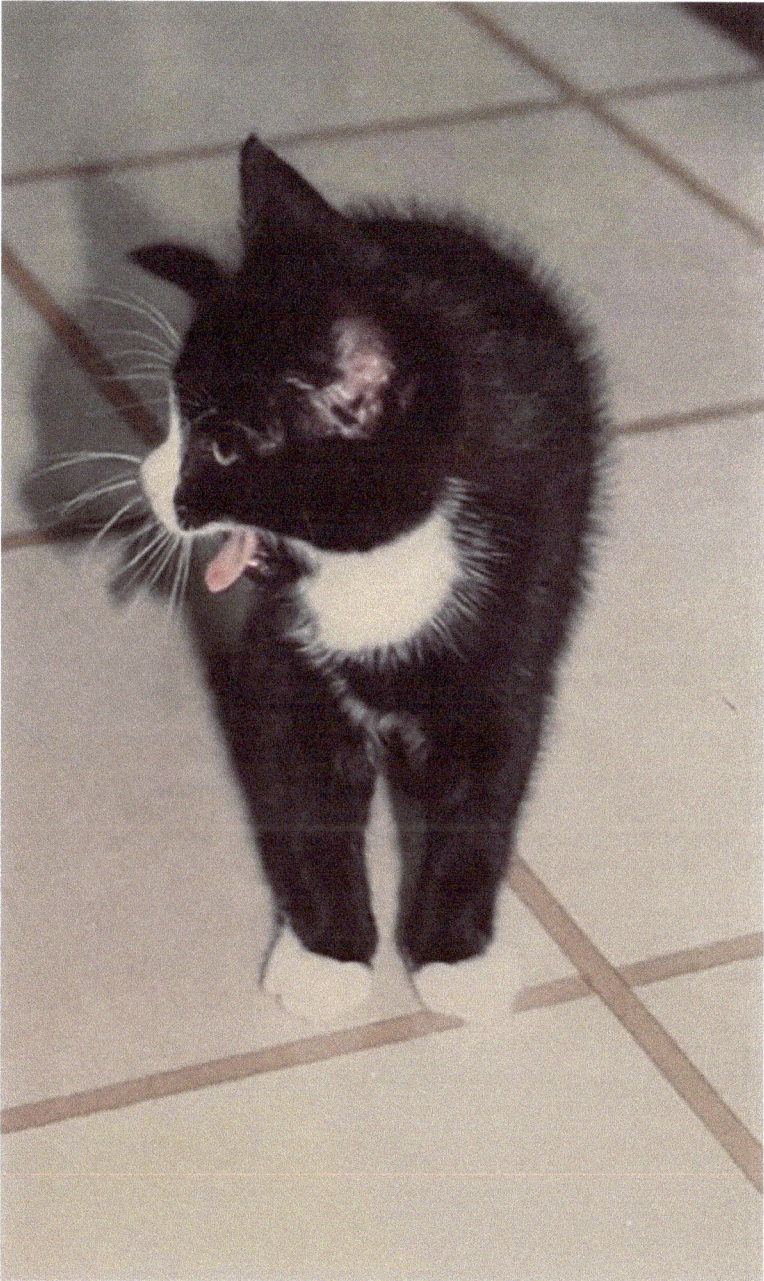

Sylvester at 3 months old

Sylvester at 7 months laying on the kitchen floor

Sylvester the kitten sitting in his bed

Sylvester at 10 years old

Sylvester fast asleep in the laundry (his bedroom)

Sylvester sees a bird as he gazes out the window on top of the stairs

Sylvester enjoying the sunshine on a Sunday afternoon

Sylvester sitting on the patio enjoying the summer sun

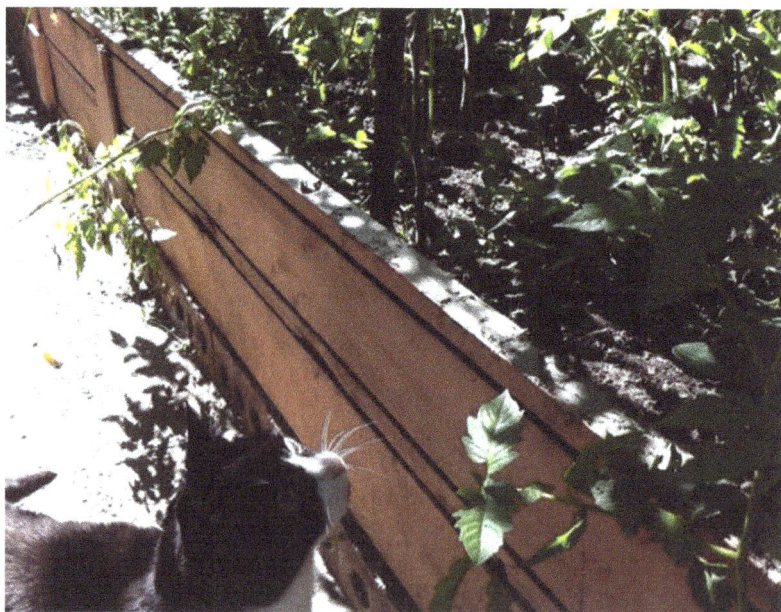

Sylvester chasing flies in the backyard

Sylvester in his bed on top of the stairs

Sylvester's favorite place to sleep. Can you see him?

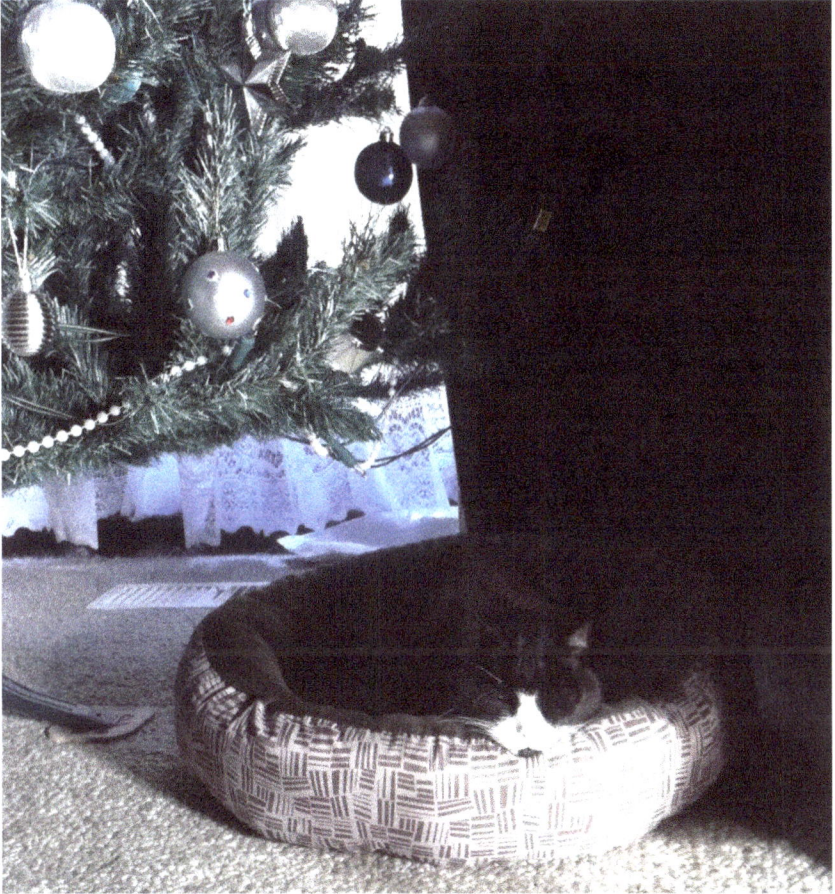

Boxing Day afternoon 2015. Sylvester was dozing off to sleep when I captured this photo

A close up of the boxing day photo. My favourite photo of him

Sylvester captivated with the decorations on the Christmas tree

Sylvester in deep thought

A cold winters day and Sylvester is rugged up as he gazes outside the lounge room window

One of Sylvester's many hiding places under the bed

Sylvester's morning routine

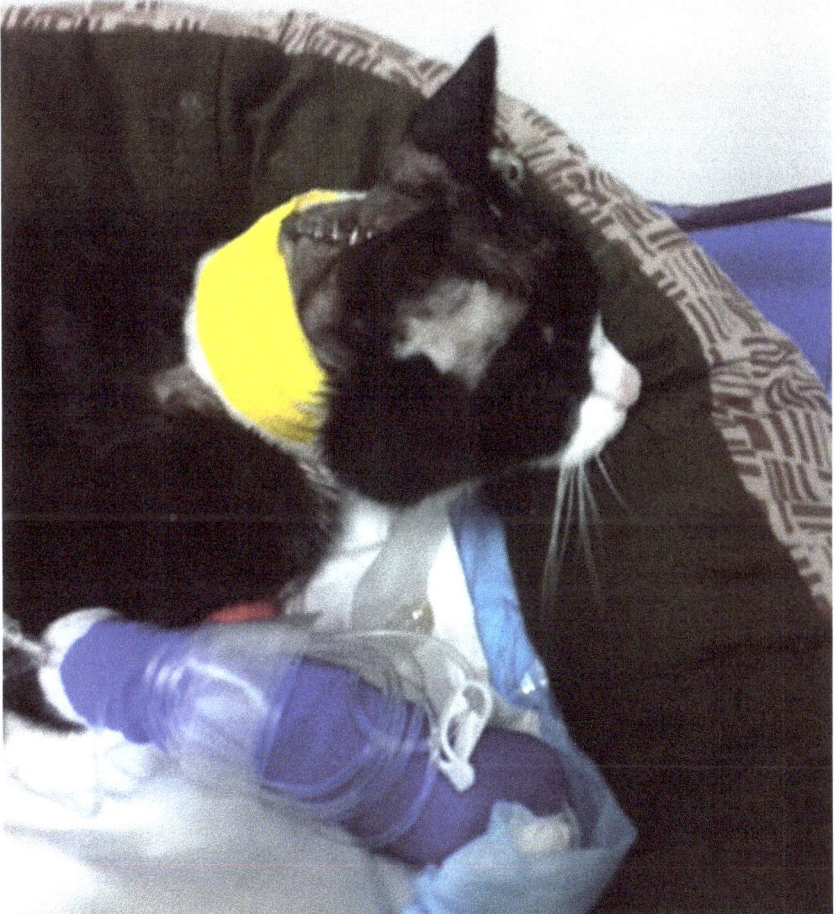

Sylvester post-op

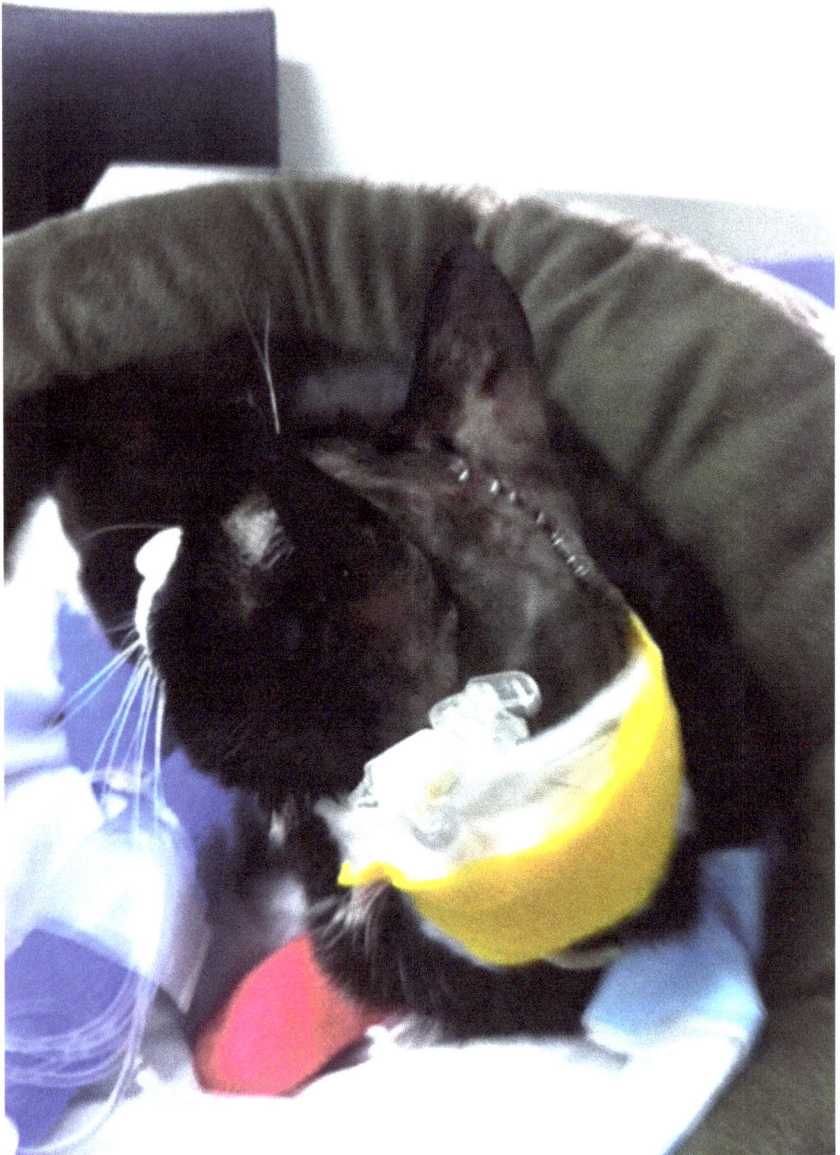

The staples show the extent of the incision. A brave cat indeed

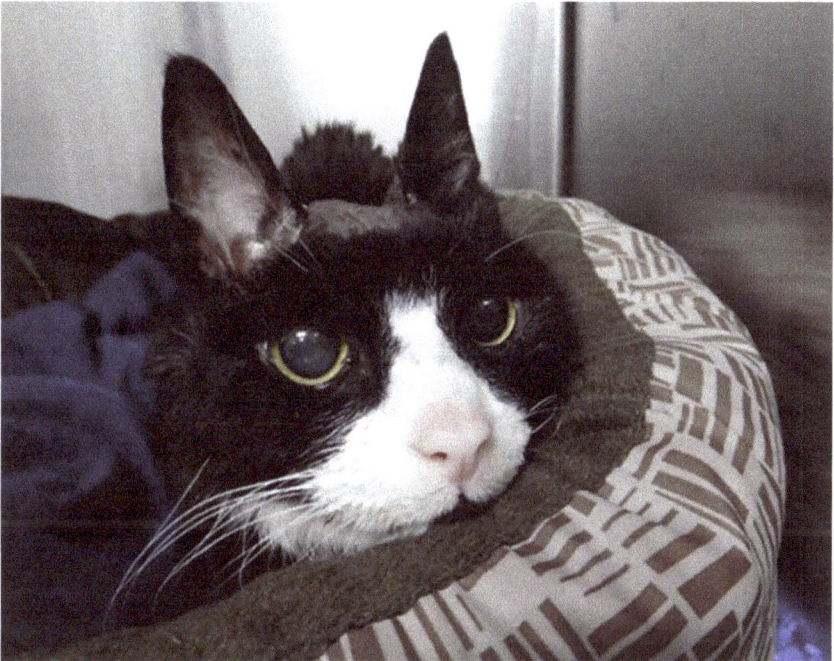

Eyes wide open after surgery. His quick recovery astonished the veterinary staff

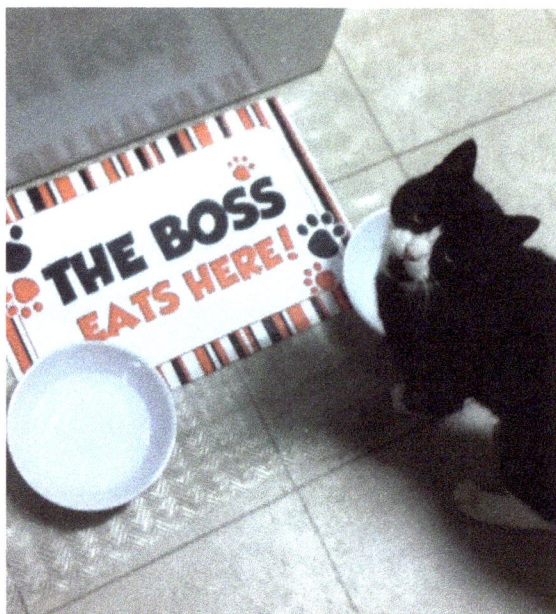

Sylvester's 24/7 diner. Always open for business

Sylvester's curiosity with flower petals

Picture Purrfect Portrait

Sylvester's pink nose a perfect hue amongst his black and white coat

Sylvester with a perfect pose as he peers out from his bedroom doorway

12

Rinse and Repeat

It was at the entrance of my bedroom that it all began. Sylvester loved to chase a thin white stick that I would wave around for him to grab. I'd take the stick from an array of plastic flowers that sat in a blue Grecian ceramic pot that adorned the upstairs hallway. When I returned it to the pot, the stick would always be half the length it was before. As soon as Sylvester was able to lock jaws on it he'd chew it relentlessly. I'd run the stick along the carpet, imitating a snake, then lift it upwards to imitate the movements of a fly, erratically flicking it through the air. Sylvester would ruthlessly chase it with the hope of catching the fictitious prey.

But on this day, almost two years after his blood transfusion and miraculous recovery, something wasn't right with him.

When he leaped for the stick, his hind legs collapsed upon contact with the floor. They weren't in sync with his front legs. I picked him up and looked to see if any debris was wedged between his paw paddings, but I couldn't see anything. I placed him back onto the floor and enticed him to grab the stick again. Each time he jumped for it he'd land awkwardly. His hind legs would tumble over and he'd collapse onto the floor. Thankfully, he didn't seem to care.

He remained absorbed by the challenge of grabbing hold of the stick. I wasn't sure if the incident was just a onetime mishap or something more sinister, so I kept a close eye on him to see if he'd do it again.

That night, Sylvester indulged in his nightly routine, playfully attacking Mum's hand. She momentarily stopped what she was watching on the television and gently grasped his belly. He curled around her hand with his four legs whilst affably gnawing her hand. His hind legs kicked up and down in rhythmic fashion. It appeared to me as if his primal instincts to capture his prey were in play; wisely, however, he understood this was playtime and not dinnertime. Sylvester's hind legs reminded me of a rabbit's, hopping in unison as it made its way to its burrow; his coordination was impeccable.

The following day I decided to take him to the local vet for a check-up and to seek some answers as to why he'd stumbled over the day before. After the consultation, the vet couldn't find anything conclusive, but if his symptoms persisted, I was to take him in again and they'd do further testing.

Two weeks later, during Christmas of 2015, I felt again that something wasn't right with Sylvester.

A week before Christmas day, I observed a peculiarity in his posture whilst he catnapped under the Christmas tree. He loved sleeping under it whenever he could do so. He'd sit in a specific position, strategically placing himself in between the various presents with his characteristic pose of all four paws tucked under his body as he sat upright. He appeared like the parcels he sat next to; perfectly square, neat and tidy, with all four corners folded impeccably.

Except on this day his head was slightly tilted to his left side. I went over and kneeled down beside him. I got his attention and in doing so was immediately shocked to see the significant misalignment of his head to his torso. There was enough evidence to suggest that something serious was wrong with him. I contacted the local vet and scheduled an appointment to have him checked over.

Upon initial assessment, the attending vet felt Sylvester may have an inner ear infection and therefore prescribed a course of antibiotics and cortisone.

After ten days of treatment, the medication appeared to have helped him... or so I thought.

I soon noticed once again his hind legs collapsing when he walked. This time his stumbling was more acute, he was falling over more frequently. His right hind leg wasn't in unison with his left hind leg, causing him to walk in a circular motion. We decided we needed answers, so we scheduled an appointment with the veterinary specialist.

The specialist examined him and suspected his symptoms could indicate something far more serious than an ear infection. Hearing this news brought back all the fears and traumas from Sylvester's past. Sylvester was exhibiting traits of a form of brain cancer in felines commonly called meningioma. Here we go again; rinse and repeat.

To confirm the vet's suspicion, Sylvester required an MRI. No matter how diligently I tried to control Sylvester's fate the uncontrollable won again. Thoughts rushed through my mind, I tried to rationalise the situation, but this time I felt a sense of disbelief rather than reassurance.

We had the MRI done immediately. It was necessary for him to be put under sedation, which in itself was nerve wracking as, at the age of seventeen and a half, there was a risk he may not come out of it alive.

I felt powerless. I was in desperate need of a dose of reassurance and guidance to deal with what was unfolding. I couldn't get over the injustice this was to us.

I nervously waited for the specialist to reach out to me with the results of Sylvester's MRI. Eventually the phone call came through on my phone. My heart was pounding at an incredible speed. My head felt light and my mouth was incredibly dry.

"Hello, Ben…"

I replied with a tone that conveyed fear and dread, "What are the results?"

He was straight to the point. Sylvester had a meningioma the size of a walnut at the base of his brain.

I hung up the phone in disbelief. Anxiety coursed through my nervous system together with shock upon hearing the results. My mind raced between hopelessness and finding a way to save him. My thoughts were scattered. What do I do now?

I knew I had to pull myself together and act. Sylvester needed me to keep my head. So I composed myself, got into my car and headed to the veterinary clinic to see Sylvester.

He came out of the sedation okay and was resting well. I was so pleased with his courage enduring the MRI scan. The specialist talked us through the MRI results of Sylvester's brain. He informed us there was one possibility for Sylvester to have any chance of survival and that was to operate on him and remove the tumour.

Realistically we had no other option other than to go ahead with the surgery. He wouldn't live for much longer if the surgeon didn't operate, and soon.

The risks were extremely high; the odds against him were mounting. The facts were confronting but required our consideration. Foremost, his mature age was not in his favour when it came to handling intricate surgery on his brain. He'd need to be under sedation for approximately two hours, a considerable amount of time and not recommended for a cat his age. But the truth was the tumour was not going away on its own. It had already grown to the size of a walnut. Comparing by the ratio of a cat's brain size to a human's, the tumour was roughly the size of a large egg.

The specialist referred us to a surgeon. The surgeon explained what he expected if he was to operate on Sylvester and the likely prognosis. Ultimately, the decision was ours to make as to whether or not to proceed.

We had no doubt what had to be done for Sylvester.

13

Seasons Change

I've got it. Yes! You're mine... darn it... no I haven't. I never seem to catch this stick.

Ben flicks a long white stick from side to side to provoke me to clasp it with my teeth. Every now and then I get the better of the stick. I clench my jaws tightly around it and then gnaw it until it breaks in two. Despite my best efforts to maul it to shreds, Ben pulls it away from me and continues to bait me by waving the last intact part of the stick.

As I jump for it, I stumble to the ground, but I immediately pick myself up. I continue to chase the stick. Oops! There I go again falling to the ground. My hind legs don't feel right.

I've noticed in recent weeks I've become clumsy, especially when I walk. And when I jump onto the sofa, I hesitate before leaping. Climbing stairs is challenging; I've lost my confidence and second-guess my steps.

I notice a tree has been assembled in the lounge room. I like this tree because there are sparkling objects that hang off its branches. I like to play with the objects, but Mum gets angry with me every time I reach for one.

As a kitten I'd attempt to climb it. As I clawed my way to the top, it would bend so I'd hastily try to climb down before it toppled over. But it frequently did. Mum would find it on the floor destroyed and she'd be furious with me. She had an uncanny ability to walk into the lounge room at just the right moment to catch me halfway up.

I'm feeling tired, so I choose to sleep under the tree. I nestle in between the paper-covered boxes that lay beneath it. Once I make myself comfortable, I doze off to sleep. I enjoy this time of the year.

I crack an eye open as Ben walks towards me. He crouches down and stares at me. He looks worried. He asks me if I'm okay; I'm not sure to be honest. I'm feeling dizzy and my vision doesn't seem okay. His appearance looks distorted almost as if he's rotated on his side.

"Why are you tilting your head?" he says to me.

I gaze at him briefly before closing my eyes.

The following morning, I awaken to the sound of the cat carrier clanking onto the floor. I'm nauseous and my head is spinning around and around. The cat carrier is out from the depths of the cellar room for one purpose only: to take me to the place for sick animals and to visit the humans in the white coats.

The trip in the car only heightens the spinning inside my head. We arrive at the vet clinic; thankfully, there are no dogs to bother me.

Ben takes me into a room and sits me on a cold steel bench. Normally I'm seen to by a lady wearing a white coat, but today a different lady is attending to me. She looks inside my mouth and ears, afterwards she chats with Ben before giving me a revolting-tasting tablet. I swallow it. She injects some medicine into the back of my neck to help with the feeling of nausea. The pain is incredible as the needle plunges into my skin, sending the medicine throughout my body. I scream a horrible meow; Ben looks distraught, as I continue to meow. He comforts me with a pat of my paw.

Shortly after this visit we arrive back home. When Ben places the cat carrier onto the kitchen floor, I quickly jump out and deliver an unfriendly growl at him for putting me through this inconvenience. I'm very annoyed at him this afternoon. I look the other direction from where he is standing and walk away to find a place of comfort. I'm annoyed for having been abruptly disturbed from my rest, and also for being confined into that clanking cat carrier. Not to mention having to endure examinations and being subjected to swallowing a tablet that tasted revolting. But what has evoked my anger most of all is having a sharp needle pricked into the back of my neck. The pain was so incredibly intense that I became very agitated and, in a fit of rage, I was primed to scratch and bite anyone close to me. However, I've been taught from an early age by Ben and Mum to never hurt my human friends. It staggers me that I'm regularly tormented with pricks from needles or prodding from examinations. I walk up the stairs and into my bed. I look around and Ben has respectfully left me alone. I see a bird outside sitting on the window sill, it's chirping at me. "Leave me alone," I meow.

Some weeks pass by and the spinning subsides. I'm able to walk without stumbling over and the nausea has almost disappeared.

Sadly, the tree with the shiny objects has disappeared as well. I notice as the weeks pass the seasons are changing. It's not as warm, so I'm inclined to find a place that is cosy, rather than to sit in the crisp air.

The leaves are falling from the trees. They've changed from a green appearance to a yellow, orange or brown colour. In my younger days, I remember chasing the leaves that fell onto the ground. I'm not inclined to chase them nowadays; I prefer to watch them through the lounge room window, from the comfort of my bed. As I peer outside, I witness the leaves dancing in the air as they dismount from their branches, landing softly on the brown dirt that surrounds the base of the tree.

I notice today the sun's rays are not as intense on my face. I hear the rustling of the wind making its way through and in between the cracks of the window. I feel it softly touch my whiskers. It's telling me it's cold outside and how lucky I am to be warm and rugged up inside.

Unlike the seasons, one constant that hasn't changed is my desire for food. Most mornings I'm starving and I meow loudly and repeatedly to get Mum's attention. She hurries over and opens the tin of food. Today I smell its chicken and pâté. Yum! I gulp it down faster than she can place it into my food bowl.

I sometimes wonder if she feeds me just to keep me quiet. I've learned from experience that the louder and longer my meows the faster I get fed. It's a clever and handy strategy I use all the time.

The next couple of days I lose my appetite, which I'd thought was impossible.

Lethargic with a splitting headache I lie down and sleep as the pain is unbearable. It feels like my head is about to explode due to pressure building up. I wish it would go away but it persists with each minute that passes, the pain becomes more intense.

Ben and Mum are by my side every minute. Ben appears to be very sad. His face is withdrawn, his eyes are heavy. I hope he's okay.

I need to close my eyes. I'm extremely tired and in a lot of pain. My head aches if I move around so I keep still, not daring to move. My head not only throbs with pain but spins around and around, making me feel nauseous. I want to vomit. I want this pain to stop.

I wish I could get up from my bed and walk around my home. I wish I could sit on Mum's lap and sleep blissfully. I wish I could play with the stick or a ball thrown down the hallway. But I'm too weary. I'm too sick.

Why is Ben crying? Oh no! Have I done something to upset him?

14

Amore Incondizionato

An unforeseen moment can put to the test your love for someone or something. For me, the test revealed itself one warm Sunday afternoon in 2006. Sylvester was eight years old.

Sylvester and I were in the backyard of our home. He relished any opportunity to chase a bird, catch a bug, or play with me. I'd roll a tennis ball down the garden path and he'd run after it. Like most cats, he was curious about the outdoors, the surroundings bombarding his senses. His instinct to hunt was apparent as soon as he'd frolic in the garden beds. I was well aware that he could take off, so I kept a close eye on him. I made sure he didn't eat anything that looked suspect. With delight he'd munch on green grass. I'd read that cats enjoyed eating grass immensely; it was comparable to candy for humans. I've also read it helps with digestive issues, something which Sylvester had plenty of experience with. The sight of me picking some grass blades from the garden sent him into a frenzy.

On this occasion, he munched down the few grass blades that had pushed their way up through the cracks in the concrete path, and I stood next to him patiently waiting for him to finish his indulgence. For no apparent reason, Sylvester decided to pounce on me. His charge was similar to a bull hurtling towards a red flag. He locked his jaws onto my lower leg, plunging his front teeth into me. As I was wearing shorts, I had no clothing to cushion the blow; his teeth pierced the surface of my calf going into the deep layers of my epidermis to almost touch my tibia bone. I screamed so loud that the next suburb could've heard my cries of pain. It was excruciating. Blood profusely dripped down my calf onto the concrete garden path.

In that moment, I recalled the last time my leg was severely wounded. It happened when I was fourteen years old. Typically after school I'd meet with friends at the local sports park just down the street from where I lived. Our pastimes were playing sports and riding bikes. On this occasion, when riding my BMX bicycle, I decided to be a little daring. I peddled up to the top of a busy road and cycled down at a reckless speed. As my velocity increased, I hit the brakes, but they didn't work. Fearing the end for me, I had to think fast; I was hurtling towards a collision and severe injury. I quickly placed both of my feet onto the unforgiving bitumen to assist with deceleration. The friction created by my shoes and the road began to heat my feet. I veered my bicycle into the adjacent street, which intersected with the road I was plummeting down. With two options available I had to decide: either crash into a neighbour's front yard that was riddled with logs and sturdy gum trees, or take a dive by turning the handlebars sharply so I'd skid, therefore creating a sudden stop. I took the latter option, but in doing so my right knee took a beating. My knee was literally skinned alive, blood and a mix of concrete stones covering the wound. Upon impact, I felt excruciating pain. My body went into survival mode, adrenalin charging through my veins. This reduced the intensity of the trauma on impact, but amplified my anger towards myself. It was the most severe leg wound I'd had until…

I look down at the blood trickling down my leg caused by Sylvester's bite. Mum came running outside to see if I was okay. I was disappointed with Sylvester, even though I believed he'd never intentionally hurt me.

Startled by my screams, Sylvester had run and hid. He wasn't able to comprehend what he'd done to me.

I searched around the garden whilst clutching my wounded leg to prevent further bleeding. Eventually I found him inside the house, hidden beneath the kitchen table. I settled him down until he was no longer scared and then I finally attended to my wound.

The sudden, uncalled-for attack should have stirred me to anger. But it hadn't. In fact, I was more concerned for Sylvester's safety than my own.

I look over my shoulder and see Ben. He's keeping an eye on me as if his life depends on it. Every move I make, he's one step behind me. Every dash I make across the pavement and into the flower beds, he's one step behind.

I'm an indoor cat, so when I venture outside and explore the backyard he's there protecting me from dangers like crossing paths with the less-than-friendly neighbour's dog or provoking a spider. "Sylvester, don't go there. Please be careful," I hear him repeatedly say to me. Today, I feel he's particularly protective and he won't let me leave his side. He doesn't understand I need space to chase the bugs and the insects, the flies and the ants. It's been way too long since the weather was fine and the critters were out so I want some hunting action. I will swipe and stun all that moves. My feline instincts are fully engaged and ready to attack.

Ben interrupts me just as I was ready to pounce on an unsuspecting spider. In frustration I turn to him and sink my teeth into his leg. I'm instantly regretful as I hear Ben scream in pain.

Overwhelmed by the error of my ways, I look for a place of refuge away from the hysteria I'd created. I'm regretting biting Ben. I hope he's okay, but I'm too scared to come out from under the table in case he punishes me.

"Sylvester, where are you? Are you okay?" he calls as he searches the garden. I can see him walk past but I'm too frightened to come out from hiding. He's holding his leg tightly, blood trickling down to his shoe.

I swallow several times, my mouth has become dry. I've done a bad thing; I've hurt Ben. I'm upset for the *pain I've inflicted on him. Maybe I should come out of hiding and accept my punishment.*

But before I get the courage to venture out, Ben finds me. I stare up at him thinking I'm in big trouble, but instead of anger I sense warmth in his voice and a genuine concern for me. He's checking to see if I'm okay. I didn't expect that. He's in pain, but instead of attending to his bleeding leg, he's attending to me. In this moment I feel guilt and shame.

I've never felt unconditional love like that except from my mother when I was a newborn kitten. She was nurturing and always by my side; she ensured that me and all my siblings were safe and well-nourished. She taught me to clean my face and to be kind to my brothers and sister. I may've been cheeky at times, but she was always there to guide me and love me for being one of her precious litter of kittens. Today I've come to understand that the love Ben has for me is the same as the unconditional love she gave me.

After a few minutes being patted and consoled, Sylvester seemed to have completely forgotten his fear and remorse. He unapologetically meowed for food. Of course he did. He had already moved on in his thoughts.

I obliged and fed him. The day's incident had put me to the test and the result was clear: my love for him was unconditional and it would remain that way.

15

Open My Eyes

I'm struggling to sleep tonight; the pounding inside my head is merciless. As I lay in my bed with no distractions from anyone or anything, I'm feeling terrified. The house is dark and eerily quiet since everyone is asleep. I'm wide-awake, staring into a dark void of emptiness. I'm momentarily comforted by a thought of sunnier days and happier times. Yet, like an uninvited party guest, the constant throbbing stands at the back of my mind with its sole focus to disrupt the broadcast of any pleasant thoughts I can muster.

At long last my eyelids draw a close to the horror story I've been experiencing tonight and I drift off to sleep...

Early in the morning the crows squawking outside wake me. I look upwards and see Ben standing by my side. He utters a soft, "Good morning, Sylvester. How are you feeling?" He pats me gently. I think he knows I'm not feeling good and by the look of his facial gestures I can tell he's worried, even though he's trying to remain positive with his reassuring words. He picks up my bed whilst I'm still huddled in it and carries me downstairs.

I can't keep my eyes open; the spinning inside my head is out of control. I feel helpless and frightened.

Eventually, my nose detects the familiar scent of disinfectant and an unpleasant dog odour. I decipher where I am. Ben talks to a lady. I hear my name mentioned a few times. Moments later, Ben kisses my forehead and then departs, leaving me behind. Fearing the worst, my body begins to uncontrollably shake. I question why he didn't take me with him. I'm confused and terrified. But I trust Ben with my life, and I must trust him now. I convince myself that he left me here for a very good reason. I hope I'm right.

A lady takes me to an enclosure that has food and water. She talks to me and tries to reassure me all is okay. I'm fatigued. My eyes remain closed as the spinning in my head is out of control. The throbbing intensifies. I can't hang on anymore, I need to let go... but I can't. I haven't said goodbye to Ben.

I'm inside an enclosure that's not spacious, it's suffocating, and I'm finding it hard to breathe. My breaths are shallow, only sufficient to gasp a small amount of air. The bright light that streams from the ceiling tries to imitate sunlight but it fails miserably. There's another cat sitting by me. She's wearing a ginger coat and has a cheerful personality. Her warm demeanour comforts me and is a timely distraction to my physical aches and the mental anguish of wondering as to the whereabouts of Ben. She says with reverence that Ben will return. She promises me that all our human parents come back to pick up their fur-babies from this place and that I'm not to worry myself unnecessarily. I thank her for comforting me.

I'm thirsty and my legs are limp. I lay splayed across the enclosure wondering when Ben's coming back to take me home.

Some hours pass and as night time ensues I hear the sound of Ben's voice. He's returned to save me! But his voice sounds unhappy. He holds my paw and I acknowledge him by clenching my claws around his finger.

"Hi Ben, I've been wondering where you have been today. I'm not feeling well. My head hurts and everything is spinning around and around."

Throughout the day, I've had my eyes closed to slow down the spinning and prevent me from vomiting. With Ben present, I take a chance to open my eyes just for one moment so I can see his face. He looks tired. He's very concerned. He speaks to the lady in the white coat for a few minutes. Both of them are looking distressed until she speaks to someone over the phone (I think it's the other vet that I go and visit), agreeing with their suggestion of a liquid that will immediately ease the fluid build-up inside my head. She grabs a needle and a clear plastic bag that contains the liquid substance. She attaches the needle to the top of my front left paw. The needle is connected to a thin clear tube that runs to the bag filled with liquid. Seconds later, I feel a strange tingling sensation run up my left leg. It travels to my chest and towards my head.

Straightaway the pressure eases inside my head and my headache subsides. After days of intense distress, I feel relief. I'm grateful for the great lengths they've gone to make me feel better. Ben is doing whatever it takes to get me back to my usual self. She gives Ben another clear plastic bag that contains the liquid substance and a drip to take home. He rugs me up in my blanket and places me in my bed. I'm finally free. Ben is finally taking me home with him.

I'm hungry, but I don't feel like getting up from my bed to eat from my bowl, so Ben and Mum feed me with a spoon. They hold the spoon to my mouth so I can lap up the milk. I try to open my mouth, but I find it difficult. My head wobbles as I reach for the spoon, but with each attempt I miss it. Ben and Mum look dejected to see me struggling. To give them some reassurance, I focus intensely on connecting my mouth to the spoon. The milk in the spoon enters my dry mouth and travels down my unquenched throat. I've been incredibly thirsty today.

I close my eyes and fall asleep.

16

The Turning of the Tide

Sylvester was now facing the greatest challenge of his life. Far greater than his internal bleeding two years prior. This beast was more ominous and a lot more brutal. I too was in a fight, a fight with my own thoughts. In one corner of the boxing ring stood optimism and in the opposing corner stood pessimism. The fight was on to see who'd reign supreme. There was no doubt whose corner I was in and I would do whatever was possible for team optimism to be standing at the final bell.

I envisaged how Sylvester might be feeling. Did he understand that he had a brain tumour? Was he frightened? Rationally, I knew he wouldn't have a clue other than the physical pain he was feeling; nonetheless, if I could have asked him these questions and listened to his response it would have given me some peace of mind. But I didn't know what he was thinking and feeling and I never will.

I could only assume that he was feeling discomfort, and as each day passed the discomfort was turning into pain. As the tumour grew it pressed on his spinal cord, affecting his motor neurons and his ability to walk and function normally.

I understood that unless he was operated on to remove the tumour he'd continue to be in great pain. He'd be suffering and in time we'd have no option but to euthanise him. It pained me to think about this last resort. But right now, there was a window of opportunity to save him.

A lot was resting on my shoulders; his life was in my hands. I was mindful of the decision I had to make, but my fears of him dying in surgery were giving me pause. I had to reason with myself that his only chance to live was for me to give the go-ahead for the operation. I considered all angles. I rationally concluded the resources and the expertise at hand, with an exceptional team of specialists and surgeon veterinarians, was first class to get the job done.

I decided we had to give Sylvester every chance in the world to survive and therefore we were going ahead with the operation. I organised to have the surgery as soon as possible. It was booked for the following Tuesday, four days away.

Sylvester had become immobile, not able to get up from his bed. I suspected the tumour was putting pressure onto the nerves of his spinal cord. In the interim prior to surgery, his dizziness, nausea and headaches were managed by medications. It was a race against time to have the operation done.

The week was a tough one emotionally. A relative had recently passed and on the day of the funeral, we had Sylvester stay at the local vet. It was the Thursday before his surgery.

That evening, I went to pick Sylvester up from the vet. Throughout the day he'd declined rapidly; his appearance was weathered, his body limp, his fur dull and matted. His condition was severe enough that the vet assistant gave me the option of euthanising him, but I couldn't authorise it. The vet, concerned for his welfare, made a call to the specialist vet for their advice. He suggested a particular medicine to be administered intravenously. It was anticipated the fluid would subside within his cranium, easing the pressure. It wasn't a cure for his headache, just a temporary relief. The cranial fluid would eventually build up again.

Moments after the vet administered a dose, Sylvester appeared to be at ease. That made me feel at ease. I picked Sylvester up from where he lay and placed him in his bed. I'd brought it along with me rather than his cat carrier. As we arrived home, I was feeling calmer than I'd been thirty minutes prior, surprising considering the circumstances. I guess my mind decided to shift gear, a means of dealing with the emotional ups and downs achieved by numbing my senses. In truth, I just wanted to get off the rollercoaster, but I had to face reality and man up. I was hoping smooth sailing would arrive soon, but I had to accept a torrential storm was heading our way. The positive was he'd made it through the day, and he was better than he was a few hours ago. It was a small win and a step forward in these trying times. Mum and I nursed Sylvester through the night. The vet provided the necessary saline to keep him hydrated, to be administered meticulously at the correct dosage at the same time on the hour, every few hours, until the surgery.

We'd planned how we'd execute the administering of the saline; we'd take shifts throughout the night after midnight so each of us could get some sleep. It was challenging, but there was no way around it. It had to be done.

Sylvester did his part by staying alive. The three days came and went and we were prepared for the biggest challenge of his life.

Tuesday morning. I had mixed emotions: on one hand I was feeling relieved that Sylvester had survived the last couple of days, but on the other I had feelings of dread for the imminent operation. That sinking feeling was with me once again and I had no other option than to confront what lay ahead with courage and positivity, regardless of how I was honestly feeling inside. In saying that, I was optimistic he had a fighting chance; his determination to fight through the pain was an indication that his will to live was unbreakable.

17

Walking on a Tight Rope

Early morning, around 8 am, we were packed and ready for the trip to the veterinary specialist centre. We'd tucked him in his bed, rugged up in his favourite blanket. No cat carrier today.

I became particularly nervous as we made the drive. The pit in my stomach was deep and it echoed with extreme uncertainty. I felt numb and a little inebriated by the anxiety. I focused on constructive thoughts. It was vital to take today step by step, to break down the day into tasks and mini goals. It was a tactic for Sylvester's success but also my way of keeping control of my emotions. Metaphorically speaking, each task was a stepping stone bridging the way to the other side of a river. The opposite bank was dauntingly far away, but if I just kept my focus on the next step and the next step, I'd make it to the other side.

Mum and I made certain Sylvester was comfortable in the consulting room. The surgeon briefed us on the potential length of surgery; approximately two to three hours. He'd be sedated for that length of time. We were aware of the high risk involved in sedating him. He was a senior cat of seventeen-plus years with a pre-existing digestive disease. He'd lost a lot of weight and had to have invasive surgery. The odds were against him to make it through the surgery, let alone for the surgery be a success.

I walked over to Sylvester and kissed him on his forehead before leaving the consulting room. A fleeting thought crossed my mind: what if that was the last time I'd see him alive? I placed my attention on something insignificant, I can't recall what in particular I focused on, whether it was the door handle to the consulting room or a dog bowl in the foyer, but whatever it was it helped redirect my thoughts and forget the unwelcome ones altogether.

My next step was to sit and wait. Sylvester's next step was to be admitted into surgery. I was spiritually with him, each step of the way. Mum and I decided it was best for both of us to head home to regain some sanity.

To distract herself, Mum kept busy with housework whilst I sat on the recliner with the remote control in hand, changing from one channel to the next, not paying attention to what was on the screen. I'd not allow any negative thoughts to ruminate in my mind, even though I was walking on a tight rope with fear and loss on either side of it. There was no way I was falling off that metaphorical rope, but frankly those few hours waiting were traumatic.

I recalled a moment a couple of days prior to the operation.

I had walked into the kitchen and unexpectedly seen Sylvester dragging himself along the floor towards the laundry. He was heading to his food bowl. It was clear to me he was determined to get there on his own. Even so, I went over to help him but as I walked closer he burst out with a meow that I translated as, "Leave me alone! I will get there myself." Upon reflection, I'm 100% certain that's what he was conveying to me. There was no other reason to meow at me in that situation.

So humbly I stepped back and let him continue on his way towards his food bowl. Slowly but surely, he dragged himself. Astonishingly, he got there.

It was the most remarkable moment I'd witnessed from him. Thinking about it in my recliner while he fought for his life in surgery, his will to live, his fight became my anchor throughout that day.

It's an example to uphold, a legacy from him that I value dearly, even today. It prompts me to push through my day whether I'm tired, unwell or feel like giving up. It inspires me to get on with life and drives me forward to keep going and to never ever give up.

Two hours passed and no news from the surgeon came. I remained seated on the recliner the entire time. I continued to distract myself by surfing the television channels, even though the hint of doom reared its ugly head from time to time. It sat with me in that black recliner chair, and like me, it wouldn't remove itself from the upholstered seating.

The familiar phone number of the veterinary specialist centre flashed up on my mobile about mid-afternoon. It rang twice before I answered. Those couple of seconds seemed to last forever. A bombardment of thoughts rushed through my mind all at once, with my heart rate racing like it was about to explode. I answered with a quivery voice, "Hello..."

The surgeon got straight to the point. He did not muddle his words; still, each syllable seemed to drag out, taking forever, and the aftermath of his statement took longer to register in my mind.

"The surgery was a success."

Once I came to my senses, the conversation only lasted a minute, although it felt much longer. I felt a wave of relief and gratitude. Sylvester had made it through a two hour operation. Unbelievable!

The surgeon was astounded by Sylvester's will to survive. The surgeon's team could not believe his ability to rebound so quickly after the operation. They'd conveyed to me he was alert and wanted to eat. *Of course, he's hungry*, I gleefully thought.

That evening, post-surgery, Sylvester recuperated whilst I had the best night's sleep I'd had in a long time. The following day, Mum and I eagerly waited to see him. I vividly recall his reaction when I walked into the consulting room. His eyes were big and bright, his head darted around looking at the surroundings and his boisterous meow was a signal he was incredibly happy to see us and likely a request for one of us to feed him.

A few days later, he was back at home. He was eating without difficulty, no more wobbling head, and he no longer required being spoon fed. He could walk without stumbling and he was able to climb the stairs without tumbling over. The back of his head was shaved so you could see his skin; he had a long scar from the top to the base of his skull that he was proudly wearing as a badge of honour. If there was a medal awarded to courageous pets before, during and after a surgery, Sylvester would be first in line to receive it.

For my part, I was grateful he had survived the operation and that he was back home and feeling okay.

18

Animals Talk

I awaken from my night's rest to the sounds of birds singing in the garden. I feel the cold air hitting my nose, although I'm rugged up and warm in my bed. Ben is asleep in his bed.

My head continues to throb, and the dizziness has yet to subside, although it's not as intense as it's been the last couple of days. I'm still lethargic, so I just lay in my bed instead of getting up. Some time passes and Ben wakes up from his sleep. The first thing he does upon waking is glance over to see if I'm okay. I move my eyes slowly in his direction and stare at him with a slow and steady gaze. I dare not move my head quickly in case the dizziness becomes overwhelming.

"Sylvester, are you okay? Today is the day we've been waiting for. It's the day of your big operation," he says softly. He picks me up and carries me downstairs. I sense it is not going to be a typical day for me.

There's no cat carrier today, instead I'm tucked in between blankets snuggled in my bed. Ben secures me in the back seat as Mum sits by my side. We're heading to the vet clinic where unwell cats and dogs visit. I've come to terms with the fact that I'm unwell and the humans are doing their best to help me get better. That said, I'm not entirely sure what's in store for me today. I'm scared, but too worn-out to meow out loud my apprehensions to Ben and Mum. Anyway, I'm not sure they'd change their mind about what they've got planned. I have no say in what's about to happen to me. I ponder my luck... is there any more remaining?

One thing is for sure, I'm lucky to have Ben and Mum in my life. They've looked after me incredibly well. Any animal that's crossed paths with loving and compassionate humans who'll take good care of them is very blessed indeed. I believe Ben and Mum are doing what's best for me today. As a result, I will let go of my fears and trust them.

The drive seems quicker than usual. I'm taken out of the car all rugged up in my bed. We enter and wait for a moment or two before heading into a room.

Once in the room, I see a table, two chairs and a bench that Ben places me on. As I sniff the air to decipher my surroundings, a man wearing a white coat enters. He greets me with a warm hello and chats to Ben and Mum; they're concerned, although I see in Ben's eyes a sparkle of optimism. I will think of him to help me through today.

Moments later they both give me a kiss on my forehead and say to me, "See you soon, Sylvester." I take a gulp and nervously lick my lips as they leave the room. Then I'm lifted from my bed by a young lady. She takes me to another room. Although I'm weary, I try to stay on guard in this unfamiliar territory.

I drift off to sleep...

I dream I'm running in the garden. I'm chasing a white butterfly as it attempts to fly away from me. I see a daffodil. It's bright yellow and smells wonderful. I hear the birds chirping; one flies over to me and says, "You're okay, Sylvester. Stay strong and enjoy the warmth of the sunshine."

My eyes open slowly; I'm feeling dazed. I partially see, with my blurred vision, a lady in a white coat standing over me. She's patting me and she's saying my name.

"Sylvester. Sylvester, how are you feeling?" she asks in a gentle voice.

I lick my lips and I look around my surroundings. The room is empty; only the lady is here with me. I feel an object around my neck. It's uncomfortable. It reminds me of the time I foolishly wedged my head inside a hole in the bedroom wall. I had been curious about what lay behind the wall, so I had decided to snoop around. I became wedged in between the plastered wall and unable to get myself out. Thankfully, through the heroics of Ben, I had been rescued. Safe, albeit embarrassed by my foolish actions.

The top of my head feels numb and the throbbing and dizziness have subsided. I'm feeling relieved. I wonder where Ben and Mum are right now.

I close my eyes, hoping when I wake, they're by my side...

I hear Ben's voice. He's talking to Mum in the next room. I'm excited because they came back for me. I'm eager to see them. They walk through the door. Ben is beaming from ear to ear. Mum looks happy and relieved.

Ben leans over and peers into my eyes. With so much joy he says, "Sylvester, how are you doing?"

I respond with a faint meow. I hope he understands I'm glad to see him.

He says to Mum, "Look at Sylvester's eyes. They're so big and wide open."

I meow at him, "What's just happened to me? And what's with this strange object around my head? It's impossible to clean my face with it on."

It's not until the next morning that I leave this place. I say goodbye to the other animals with whom I've become friends in my time here. Some of them have strange cones around their heads. I wonder if that's the object

I have on my head? They look ridiculous. I hope I don't look as silly as them.

A ginger cat that looks a lot younger than me gives me a glance and says with a tone of kindness and admiration, "We all thought you wouldn't make it through the operation. We're astonished by how well you've recovered. All the animals yesterday spoke about your bravery, including the disgruntled brown kelpie sitting over there in the kennel. He wouldn't stop barking. He was so excited to hear the good news about you this morning. We all wish you safe travels in your journeys."

Feeling overwhelmed and bashful for the kind words the ginger cat has spoken, I say my goodbyes to all my new friends and wish them well on their journeys too. I see Ben and Mum waiting for me in the foyer. One of the ladies picks me up in my bed and takes me to them. They're smiling with joy as I'm going home with them today.

In the following days I begin to feel more energetic, no longer plagued by the persistent throbbing and dizziness that robbed me of my vitality. I'm up and about, no longer confined to my bed; I'm eating food and drinking water without the need to be spoon fed. I walk without stumbling; I'm able to climb the stairs without stopping midway to recollect my balance. I take pleasure in sniffing the floor, the air and the food aromas in the kitchen. I'm excited to gaze outside and watch the birds building shelter for the bitter cold winter that is on our doorstep.

I walk past the wall that once had the hole in it but has now been repaired. Momentarily, I ruminate about my recent entrapment, grateful that I no longer have the strange object around my head. I'm able to clean my face for the first time in a long time. However, I detect an unusual sensation when I groom myself. As I sweep along the top of my head with my paw, I can't feel fur but rather a line of tender raised skin that now sits there instead.

19

Walk Before You Fall

One week after his brain surgery something unexpected happened.

I was relaxing on the recliner when Sylvester casually strolled past me. I reached down to pick him up from the floor but he walked a little faster to escape my clutches. He was clearly not interested in me; he only cared to watch the outside activities from the lounge room window.

As I let go of him and watched him stroll off towards the window, to my surprise, his hind legs collapsed just like they had done prior to the operation. A moment of confusion crossed my mind. What had just happened?

Symbolically, the recliner seemed to always play an extra in the story of Sylvester provoking uncertainty... it's time to get rid of it!

Many years ago, when the doorbell sounded, Sylvester would scurry to find a place to hide. He'd more often than not find a place of refuge behind the lounge room sofas. There he'd sit patiently until it was safe to come out. He'd learned as a kitten that when the doorbell rang, humans would be circling his domain and, apart from his human family, other humans were a potential threat to him.

We'd become accustomed to Sylvester hiding every time the doorbell rang. If we knew people would be visiting, we'd let them know to not ring the doorbell and then we'd spend the next minute or so explaining why. Knowing his hiding place, I'd leave the sofa a little bit away from the wall, so he'd be able to hide comfortably within the dark underside of it. I'd notice after the visitors left that Sylvester would cautiously come out of hiding. He'd meow boisterously, demanding food; I'm sure he was expecting us to feed him after we'd inconvenienced him enough to hide.

I got up from the recliner and inspected his legs. I had him walk around the lounge room and observed his hind legs stumbling as they had before.

Had the tumour returned? Had the surgeon left some of the tumour behind and it had regrown? I had no idea why he was stumbling and I was overwhelmed as to what to do now.

The following day we booked an appointment for Sylvester to see the veterinary surgeon. It was concluded that Sylvester had to have another MRI to determine what was going on within his head. He'd already been through enough traumas but unfortunately it needed to be done.

Both the specialist and the surgeon believed it was highly unlikely the tumour had grown back in such a short period of time—it had only been a week!—but the MRI would show if this was the case or not.

Sylvester had to go under sedation again. This was becoming all too much for me. But I had to remain positive and focused. *It's just a routine check*, I thought to myself. *Sylvester has been through so much unfortunate luck that this surely cannot be more of the same.*

That evening, I drove to the veterinary specialist centre, my heart beating uncontrollably. The surgeon was due to call late that afternoon, but I wanted to hear the results in person. Before I arrived, the surgeon's call came through on my phone.

"No evidence of a tumour," the specialist said. He assumed it was most likely inflammation from the tumour that was affecting Sylvester's motor skills. I breathed a sigh of relief. I arrived at the clinic, picked Sylvester up and we headed home.

There was no improvement in the ensuing days. Further tests had to be done. The specialist performed a biopsy of his brain, extracting fluid to determine if it was just inflammation. A godsend was that he didn't have to go under sedation. A sample could be taken from the part of his skull that had been operated on; the vet could easily extract some brain fluid for testing.

The results came back... The news was horrid. Sylvester had brain lymphoma.

In his research, the specialist had found only one other case in the world, some thirty years ago, where a feline had had two different types of brain cancer. It was that uncommon. It was that unlucky and it was very unfair.

Sylvester could receive chemotherapy or remain on steroids, but there was no cure for this type of cancer in animals.

I was disconsolate, incredibly empty inside and emotionally drained. I looked at Sylvester and wondered if he had any idea what was going on within his body. I guessed he didn't understand and that made me feel all the worse. I could see his fate, but he'd not any clue or even a care in the world. He carried on as usual. I supposed it was better that way; him not knowing or understanding the ramifications of the news.

I struggled to remain positive that evening. The heartbreaking news was devastating. Part of me was wishfully thinking he'd defy medical prognosis and be restored to good health. I would just need to continue with the strategies that had seen him through the previous times and pray that miraculously he'd be healed.

I decided to put my emotions aside and get on with the treatment for him…

20

Winter is Coming

After devouring my afternoon snack of tasty pieces of turkey and gravy, I consider my choices for afternoon entertainment. It's a relaxing Sunday afternoon and I desire some amusement. I decide to survey the outside world from the lounge room window and to behold the usual suspects in the backyard, such as the bird that wears a grey feathered coat and a bright yellow beak, who sings with regularity at the same time each day. And the vegetable garden and the array of insects hovering around the barren stems that yearn for the presence of the vegetables that accompanied them last summer. And the sun peeking through the grey clouds, but only for a moment, before vanishing behind the ominous dark rain cloud making its way from the bay.

They're the main characters of a stage spectacle that's on show and I'm fortunate to have a front row seat. To get to my vantage point, I need to bypass Ben who's relaxing in the recliner chair. Past experience tells me he'll grab me and sit me on his lap. But today I'm planning to escape his clutches and go sit to watch the afternoon matinee special. I've only one way of getting past him. Slyly, I walk towards the window, hoping to not gain his attention. As I make my way past the recliner chair, I watch his hands reach over, heading in my direction. I make a quick stride or two and evade his clasp but in doing so my hind legs misstep and I fall to the ground. I pick myself up and continue to walk towards the window. I glance over my shoulder to see if he looks like he is planning to grasp me a second time, but he doesn't. Instead he looks baffled. I'm surprised by his reaction but continue on my way to the window.

He takes one of the long white sticks that sit in the vase next to the recliner and starts waving it in front of me. Instinctively, I stop walking and jump for it. In doing so, I tumble over onto the floor. He waves it again and again and I fall over each time. After a few more failed attempts, he stops waving it and lets me continue on my way to the window. I'm annoyed with him; he always wants to play with me when I have other plans. Though today I'm uncertain as to why I can't jump and land on all four paws. I feel no pain in my legs. The headache that I had a few weeks ago is no more; in fact, I feel great. I get to the window and make myself comfortable in front of it.

It's morning and after gulping down my breakfast serving of fresh chicken and gravy, I walk to my usual place at the top of the stairs. Glancing towards the front entrance, I see a conspicuous object. It's covered with a green and white chequered tablecloth. I know what hides underneath. Ben and Mum can't fool me. It's the cat carrier unceremoniously waiting for me.

To avoid its clutches, I seek refuge at the top of the stairs. However, to get to them I must pass the cat carrier. I begin my walk, stealthily making my way past it and towards the base of the stairs. My first step is a tad wonky; I seem to find my front legs are a mismatch for my hind legs. I gradually make my way to the top stair; I pause for a moment and then change my plan of escape. I decide its best for me to hide under Ben's bed—it's my go-to place to hide. I'll wait here until the coast is clear and the cat carrier has gone back to the cellar dungeon. I gulp. I hope Ben doesn't find me under here.

"Sylvester!" Ben exclaims.

I see his face as he peers under the bed. I'm sitting as far back as possible against the wall. I'm a great deal smaller than him so it's a struggle for him to get under the bed and grab me. But on this occasion he's quick, and before I can escape to another refuge he grabs me, takes me downstairs and places me inside the cat carrier. I meow at him, demanding he let me out. Unfortunately, what I've learned over the many years of meowing for my release is that it's always in vain. Even so, I continue to meow loudly, expressing my displeasure for being confined inside it. Until I'm sitting in my bed comfortable and undisturbed, I will stubbornly persist with my meowing.

I'm distracted by the smell of disinfectant and the odours from other cats and dogs wafting from the entrance of the vet clinic. Ben takes me inside and I stop my vocal protest. The surroundings capture my attention. I raise my nose and sniff the air. We walk into a room as a man in a white coat says hello. Ben and Mum start talking to him whilst he observes how I walk around the room.

I best show him how wonderfully I can walk! I circle around and walk up and down the room. Can you see how perfect I walk now?

Unfortunately, they observe me walking clumsily; my hind legs are dragging along the floor like they did once before. Now I'm worried... what's wrong with me? Will they still love me if I keep stumbling over? I'm trying so hard to be the best cat for them but I'm letting them down. I'm letting myself down. I'm a disappointment. But I won't let them know how I feel. I will pretend everything is fine and that this mishap is nothing for them to be concerned about. I don't want to be seen as a problem. I couldn't think of anything more undignified than being a burden to my family, to Ben and Mum, who have cared for me for nearly eighteen years of their lives. They've sacrificed so many things for me; I can't let them down now. I continue to prance around the room, still trying to regain my prowess, showing no sign to them of what I'm feeling in this moment.

Ben and Mum leave me with the man in the white coat so he can do further tests on me. Before he does, I wait in a room that is occupied by other animals. It's the same room I stayed in a few weeks ago.

I look for the ginger cat and the barking dog but they're not here. Instead, I see a white rabbit and a light brown mouse in cages in the corner. The rabbit is asleep whilst the mouse is scurrying around inside its cage.

My friends from the last stay aren't here, but some things never change. There's always the incessant yapping of a dog. Today there are two seeking attention. Sitting near me is a cat; she has a grey coat with a white face and paws. She looks very unhappy.

She nods at me and says, "Hello, nice to meet you. How are you?"

"I'm good, thank you. I'm here for a quick visit. Why are you here?"

"I've had to have my tummy checked by the people in white coats. I've been here for a couple of days. I'm missing my home."

I respond kindly, "Don't worry. Before you know it you'll be home, cuddled up warm and feeling happy again."

It's nice to see another cat amongst these noisy dogs. I take a deep breath and sigh. Not long after, I doze off to sleep.

I awaken to see Ben and Mum standing over me. I meow at Mum to let her know I'm hungry and then glance over at Ben. He seems anxious. On the way home I hear him talking with Mum. He's talking about me as she just listens.

Oh boy, what have I done now? I'll make it up to them tonight after I eat my dinner. I'm heading straight for Mum's lap to snuggle up and keep her warm. And later I'll spend some time sitting with Ben whilst he pats me.

21

Flies That Buzz

Time is fleeting, I think back to when I was a kitten, full of vitality and mischief. I'd race up and down the stairs and around the house. Nothing could catch me. My nimble legs accelerated to top gear when I heard the tin can being opened. As the tasty chicken pieces tumbled into my food bowl, I'd already be sitting next to it. As soon as the food landed in the bowl, I'd be guzzling it down my throat.

Nowadays when I hear the tin can, I walk at a steady pace so as not to aggravate the aches and pains that I now endure in my old age. Experience has taught me there's no need to rush to my bowl; the food will be sitting in it when I finally make my way to it.

It's not that I've become lazy, I just recognise that conserving energy is important. It was only recently, in the days before my brain surgery, that I'd mustered up an act of incredible strength. It was late in the evening and I had been feeling peckish. I'd left some food in my bowl from dinner. Regrettably, my legs hadn't had the strength to take me from the lounge room to my food bowl in the laundry. Tired of feeling helpless, I had decided to slither to my food bowl. With the use of my two front legs and my razor-sharp claws, I had dragged myself along the lounge room carpet then onto the tiled kitchen floor. Inch by inch, I drew closer to my food bowl, now only metres away.

At the time, Ben had walked into the kitchen. His immediate reaction had been to try to pick me up and carry me to my food bowl. But I'd abruptly meowed at him, demanding to be left alone. I hadn't needed his help that time round. He had reacted by taking a step backwards, but his eyes had remained fixed on me. Through the corner of my eye, I had seen his facial expression. I could tell he was in awe of me. He couldn't believe my act of strength.

"I won't let you down, Ben. I promise. Stand back and watch me do this all by myself," I meowed.

I managed to get to my food bowl. I'd slithered like a snake for at least five metres. On the topic of food bowls...

I've noticed that whenever I have tummy issues and I've visited the lady in the white coat, I discover, in the days following, small white tablets hidden in my food bowl in between chunks of tuna. I never understood their purpose but I knew they had been deposited by either Ben or Mum. I could only assume their intention was to make me feel better. Nevertheless, the taste did not reflect that; they were bitter and unsavoury. They were typically hidden inside a portion of the meat pieces slobbered with gravy, strategically placed at the bottom of the bowl. I could acknowledge the monumental efforts taken by Ben and Mum to disguise them. Little did they realise I could smell them, so camouflaging the pills from my sight didn't work.

Mum would say, "Sylvester! I can't believe you ate the food but left the tablet!"

I would walk away licking my lips and staring at her blankly. I'm dumbfounded as to why she thinks she can fool me.

In the weeks following my walk to the window incident, my hind legs have been working just fine. Even so, my weekly routine of visiting the vet remains unchanged. We're greeted by the same man in the white coat who talks with Ben and Mum. He has me chase a piece of string to observe my coordination. Depending on my mood; I either chase it or spitefully stare at the wall. Today he's discussing with Ben and Mum what he thinks is best for me. I'm guessing the topic of conversation is the most appropriate tablet for me to take; with a snigger I think to myself, *No chance of that happening!*

I look up at the fluorescent light; there's a fly buzzing and seeking attention. The animals and insects in this place want to be heard. I just want to get out of here and go home.

22

Rose-Coloured Glasses

Treatment started immediately for Sylvester. Steroids were prescribed to help contain the spread of the lymphoma, but sadly they wouldn't cure it. For now, they remained the most appropriate course of treatment. Eventually chemotherapy would be required. As to when, that depended on how long the steroids could keep the lymphoma at bay.

I was struggling to comprehend the unfairness of it all. But as with each sickness Sylvester had met, I decided that I'd be unwavering. Whatever was within my control I would do. I researched the current treatments available and developed a greater understanding of lymphoma in felines; additionally, I sought out the latest advanced therapies available and whether they'd be suitable for him.

When Sylvester was diagnosed with meningioma, I had researched as much as I could about the disease. I had studied numerous academic papers so I could be familiar with current treatments. I would bring that same intensity to researching lymphoma in felines.

I was dedicated, but heartbroken. The continuous battle was wearing me thin. It was only a few weeks ago that he'd overcome a brain tumour. I imagined a sliding doors moment: instead of him stumbling that Sunday afternoon he'd dash past me with an impeccable gallop. But as quickly as I'd fantasised about this ideal situation, reality pried its way back into my mind and that sinking feeling took a firm hold. Marshalling myself to take control of my fear, I refocused on the task at hand; it was wasteful to do otherwise.

Sylvester had regular blood tests to determine the progress of the lymphoma. After a few weeks of treatment with cortisone, a blood test confirmed the lymphoma was under control. Incredibly, he was in remission.

The specialist and his team were in awe of Sylvester's fight to live; his immune system had the doggedness to pacify the cancer in its tracks. For now, he was in control of this battle. I chose at that moment to ignore the prognosis that was given weeks before. For me, ignorance was bliss.

But just as quickly as good news arrived at our doorstep it departed, slamming the door shut behind it. The following week, I noticed Sylvester's hind legs looked very swollen; they looked like they'd been filled with air, like balloons. Initially I thought the swelling could have been a common reaction to the medication. I immediately called the specialist vet. He said that the lymphoma could not be beaten and it was now starting to take over Sylvester's body. The swelling was a perilous indication the disease was fighting back.

With the progression of the disease, the specialist used a range of medications to control the swelling and for a couple of days it subsided. Sadly it returned, insidiously moving to his front legs and abdomen.

The truth was the steroids were being overpowered by this horrible disease; the alternative was chemotherapy. We'd been cornered in the metaphoric boxing ring with this monster attempting to give the final knockout blow. Our last hope for Sylvester to outfox this onslaught was chemotherapy. We decided to go ahead with the treatment.

I wished I had a magic wand so I could cure him; I wished it had not come to this.

The specialist said there was an array of chemotherapy medicine available, but he felt one in particular would be less intrusive for Sylvester. For the first twenty-four to forty-eight hours of treatment, Sylvester would be highly toxic and his urine or faeces could be toxic to humans. Wearing of gloves and applying the utmost attention to detail with cleanliness needed to be adhered to; we'd follow the specialist's instructions and ensure nothing would go amiss.

The following Saturday was the first day of his treatment. Prior to heading to the specialist vet, we took a trip to see a holistic vet who was renowned for using both eastern and western medicine for animals.

I often think about the way Sylvester looked on the way there. Peaceful and content, he had watched the surrounding sights through the car window, his head darting from one visual to another. Watching him at the time, I was sad. It was all too much for me and I believed it must have been for him as well.

The following Monday, some forty-eight hours after his first dose of chemotherapy, Sylvester was very subdued; he'd not moved out of his bed all day, his nose had gone pale, his paws were limp. I was scared. To add to my worries, the gas and electricity had gone out at home. Night had fallen early; it was dark and cold with no lighting or heating available.

At that moment I felt the depths of despair and ghastly horror for Sylvester. The situation was bleak. Everything looked to have crashed to the ground around him.

Throughout the next week I spent a lot of time sitting by his side. He rarely moved out of his bed. His legs and abdomen were swollen, his face looked exhausted. I pondered what was going through his mind. His scar stood out more than ever in the morning sunlight. It was slowly healing, but the rest of his body was not. He no longer bothered to look outside the window to watch the birds, the trees or the ants scurrying along the concrete, and he no longer cared to play with the stick from the blue pot at the top of the stairs. I reminisced about the past with him. I dared not think about a future without him.

Throughout the morning I never left his side. I held him, guiding the plastic spoon towards his mouth so he could drink from it. I mushed up some chicken, but he didn't want to eat it. I was doing the best I could possibly do for him. He gazed into my eyes; I could see every detail of his pupil. It was big and bright, just like the morning sun that shone upon it. He conveyed an unspoken message to me that I've done more than enough. It's more than he can ever thank me for today, and for his entire life.

On Sunday night, a week after his first chemotherapy session, he lay motionless in his basket. I decided to sleep by his side that night. I took him up to my bedroom where I placed him next to my bed.

I had an awful dream, horrific to say the least. I dreamt I was in a boat sailing the deep blue sea. In the distance, thunderstorms beckoned. The winds howled and the rain pelted down from the heavens. There was a hole in the hull of the boat. I endeavoured to patch it but to no avail. The boat started to sink. I was alone and helpless. The boat submerged into the icy waters.

Throughout the night I woke frequently, checking on Sylvester each time. Each time he'd look at me as if he was trying to tell me something.

Morning arrived; he was motionless in his bed. He had an appointment to see the specialist vet, so we had to get him ready for the trip. The specialist was not attending that morning, so his assistants were to check Sylvester over.

I picked him up in his bed and carried him down the stairs to the laundry, his bedroom for the last seventeen and a half years. Mum had placed some food in his bowl. He nibbled a few pieces before walking to his kitty litter.

Upon picking Sylvester up from the laundry floor he kicked his hind legs in protest; his right hind leg scratching me lightly on the inside of my right wrist. I've never forgotten that scratch.

I placed him in his bed and we headed outside to Mum's car. I opened the passenger side door and placed Sylvester on the seat, making sure he was snug and warm in his bed. We'd decided that Mum would take him to the veterinary specialist centre this morning, as I had meetings scheduled at work. I closed the door, observing him snuggled up in the blankets.

I climbed into my car and followed Mum to the main road where the peak hour traffic was heavy with commuters on their way to work. Mum got a break on the main road and I missed getting behind her. She was in the distance. The next main traffic lights were green, so I drove straight ahead whilst Mum made a left turn, heading in the direction of the veterinary specialist centre. I looked to my left driving through the intersection. I saw the back of her car in the distance making its way.

23

Pen and Paper

It's a cloudy Sunday afternoon and I am lying in my bed next to the recliner chair where Ben sits. In one of his hands is a pen and in the other a notebook. He's fatigued and in deep thought, but he continues to write. He raises his head and glances over at me; I catch his stare, our eyes lock. I briefly close my eyes to break the connection because I can't bear to see him so sad.

I knew the day our paths crossed that I'd found my human friend for life. He's forever perfect for me as I know I am for him. Many animals across the planet are not as fortunate as me; they don't have a loving home and are left to suffer and be mistreated. I've been one of the blessed animals and for that I'm eternally grateful.

Ben stops writing for the moment to come see how I'm doing. I muster up the strength to raise my head to let him know I'm doing okay. I take a deep sigh and lay my head back onto the blankets which have been keeping me warm. My ears remain alert to the sounds of my surroundings, even though I feel safe and protected with Ben by my side. Soon I will need to let go... but not today.

Evening arrives. It's cold and typically wintery outside. Darkness sets in a lot earlier at this time of the year. My days and nights blur into one. I no longer desire to look outside and watch my friends in their daytime folly; the birds, the insects, and the trees are all but a memory now. My eyes no longer care to scope the backyard for their scope is front view only. My ears have never let me down and have now taken over authority from the other senses to alert me to changes in my surroundings.

Ben has taken on the role of my eyes. As my guardian angel, he watches over me with unconditional love. He is my protector from the world around me.

My eyes water at the thought of what lies before me and how Ben will cope without me. God tells me all will be okay, but I find it hard to believe that right now.

I sleep next to Ben's bed whilst tucked up and cosy in mine. I feel his energy. He's in utmost despair and I'm helpless to make him feel better. The only thing that will ease his worries is for me to get better.

I've tried so much to stay strong, but I was not created to live forever, none of us were. Ben logically understands this, but I know he wishes it were not the case.

Throughout the night, he regularly checks on me. Each time he does, I raise my head and glance at him, signalling all will be okay. I want him to go to sleep and rest. I want him to be happy, but I realise his happiness depends on me becoming better. Yet I feel like I'm at sea, caught in a current that's determined to pull me away from the shoreline. It's increasingly hard to sustain my energy. The water's edge is escaping me. I'm too exhausted to swim any longer.

The morning sunshine breaks through the window as I lie rugged up in my bed. I hear the birds chirping, their sounds are reassuring. Sometime after I hear Ben wake up. He looks at me from his bed as he rises and asks me how I'm doing. He picks me up, still huddled in my bed, and takes me downstairs to my room where my food bowl sits. It hasn't been used for some time.

I see Mum finishing off a piece of toast and a cup of freshly brewed coffee for breakfast. Normally I'd cry out to her to feed me, but this morning I'm not hungry. I sense I'm heading to my weekly check-up at the vet. My belongings are packed for our trip. Ben picks me up from the floor; I accidently scratch his right inner wrist as he places me back into my bed. No cat carrier today, only my bed with blankets to keep me warm from the frosty air.

Ben makes certain I'm secure and safe in the passenger side of the car. Today Mum is taking me for a check-up; Ben is unable to be by my side on this visit. I sense he's looking over me as I curl up, protected from the cold. Ben says goodbye.

I can't see his face as he closes the car door. I sigh...

24

Message in a Bottle

Throughout the morning I received phone calls from Mum and the vet's assistants. Sylvester was not good at all. I cried in the corner of my work office, trying to compose myself. I was at work and not by his side where I should be. I'd been by his side every step of the way, but not now. He seemed okay when I'd seen him hours earlier. What was going on? What were they doing to him?

By midday I decided to head to the veterinary clinic to see him. I couldn't be away from him any longer. I was numb and lightheaded. I felt nauseous and scared to death.

I got into my car and just as I pulled out of the driveway my phone rang. It was the veterinary clinic's phone number on the screen.

I felt a little dizzy as the cortisol coursed through my veins. My chest tightened and it became harder to breathe.

I answered…

The instant the kitten's large green eyes connected with the human's hazel eyes there was a kindling of souls. It was as if destiny had called and serendipity answered.

But just as unexpectedly as the human had appeared at the window he disappeared. The little black and white kitten sighed and, as all kittens love to do, he nodded off to sleep...

The specialist asked if I was driving. I said I was, but I'd pull over. He waited silently until I did so.

I'll never forget that spot on the side of the street where I parked my car. It was under a parking sign, trees overhanging the curb, the sun had broken through the midday clouds.

"I have to let you know, Sylvester passed away this morning. We did everything we could."

Frozen and in complete shock, I cried and cried and cried. I've never felt such pain as I did in that moment.

I knew this day would inevitably come, but I hadn't imagined it would be that day and in that way. I wasn't there for him. I didn't say goodbye.

Unfortunately, the specialist wasn't there either. I didn't know who had attended to him. I didn't know what had happened. The pressure on my heart was unbearable. I went home and I cried some more.

The monster had won the fight.

Before I close my eyes of a night and fall asleep, I ask Sylvester to visit me in my dreams and invariably he does. He looks well, happy and youthful. I awaken feeling at peace, recollecting the dreams of holding Sylvester and watching him play in the garden. I feel somewhat melancholy yet overwhelmed with love and grateful that I had an opportunity to rekindle the friendship we'd shared in physical form.

Today my days are spent moving forward in my life; nonetheless, every day I feel the sorrow of Sylvester not being around me. I miss him dearly. Sylvester taught me many virtues: balance, unconditional love, courage and companionship to name a few.

To this day, I find new ways to survive his loss. One way has been to put pen to paper by telling his story and keeping his memory alive. I know time heals all wounds, but the scar will always remain.

I talk to Sylvester all the time. I look for signs regularly. I believe he hears me. I believe that first week after his passing he reached out to me. I slept in his room and every night I beckoned him to give me a sign. Literally seconds later, a baby possum was at the bedroom windowsill, scratching to come in. No possum had ever come to that window in my forty years living there. To add, it appeared straight after I'd asked Sylvester to show me a sign. I'd like to believe it was him instructing the possum to say hi for him. It helps me feel at ease that he may still be around me in spirit.

Some weeks later, I asked Sylvester to show me a clear sign that he was doing okay, wherever he may be in spirit. To my surprise, a couple of hours later a sign came. I opened my top bedroom drawer, a drawer I frequently opened, and a photo sleeve full of photos popped right out from under an array of papers. Until then, I'd never thought to open the photo sleeve to see what was inside. But on this occasion, the photos jumped out of the photo sleeve staring at me front and centre. They'd been sitting in my drawer for many years. Poignantly, these were photos of Sylvester as a kitten and they were the missing pieces of the collage of photos I was collating of him at the time.

I hope Sylvester visits me tonight in my dreams. I hope he tells me that he still loves me and he is so thankful for everything I did for him and that he could not have asked for a kinder, more caring and loving friend than me.

I know that when times are tough I can call on his fighting spirit.

I love you, Sylvester, for ever and ever. You are *Forever Perfect*.

This is my story through the eyes of Ben. I know I'm not forgotten.

Today as Ben writes this passage, my memory lives on. It's exactly, to the day, four years since I said goodbye to him.

He talks to me a lot. He's kept my bed and my teddy bear and he remembers me by the photos he has taken of me and him. He even still has the cat carrier. He misses me, I know that for sure. He kisses a photo of me sitting under the Christmas tree every morning and night.

He talks to me as if I'm there with him. I'm there every time he thinks of me.

I'm so grateful to have had a loving friend in Ben.

"Sometimes a very special cat enters our lives... their presence changes our hearts forever. And we can call ourselves blessed for having known them."
Unknown

Purr-spective:
Sylvester's Message for You

To you, the reader, thank you for allowing me to come into your life through the pages of this book. If I can offer you a guiding paw, then this is what I'd like to personally share with you:

Animals are your best friends and we'll always be loyal to you. Whether we're a dog, a bird, a mouse, a fish, a rabbit or a black and white cat, we'll be there for you even when you're not always there for us.

We adore you and we think you're the greatest. We'll wait at the front door for you to come home and we'll sit on your lap and hug you heaps if you allow us to do so.

When you're busy getting on with your daily tasks and responsibilities, please don't overlook us, standing in the corner, wishing for your attention. Just come over and pat us, and if you take notice, you'll see a gleam in our eyes of gratitude that you did so.

We'll express unconditional love, forgiveness, compassion, loyalty and reliability throughout our lifetime with you. Qualities we hope you carry forward in your life as an example to uphold. They're our gift to you.

As tough as this is to accept, you'll most likely outlive us. And for some of us, we'll be faced with injury or illness during our lifetime. We love you so much and we like to believe you love us just as much and, if we're to fall ill or get injured, you'll take good care of us. I know the humans in white coats do their very best to care for us when we're sick or injured. If you're dealing with or have dealt with a sick or injured pet, or sadly lost a beloved animal friend, please remember one important thing—you're never alone. We'll always be by your side, even when we're no longer in physical form. Our love will comfort you in times of need and your thoughts of us will keep us forever alive. Embrace us again, just like you embraced us into your life when we were in physical form.

"Life is a series of hellos and goodbyes." A lyric by Billy Joel. It's relevant to all relationships; human and animal alike. But in searching for a lifetime love, a hello is a risk worth taking.

I hope my story provides you with inspiration and I wish you and your animal friends the most prosperous lives.

If you ever need encouragement, think of me and my journey.

Sylvester

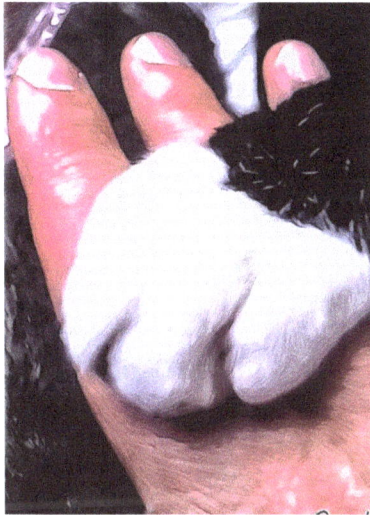

About the Author

Benito Cossari is the author of "The Ant and You", an Aurora House publication. He has twenty-five years' experience in the corporate world, coaching people to become the best version of themselves. He holds a Bachelor of Business Degree, an Associate Diploma in Marketing and a Cert. IV in Fitness. His other passion is art. He's painted numerous works with a catalogue of drawings and canvas paintings.